Dead End Donation

A Laugh-out-loud Small-town Mystery

Kirsten Weiss

MISTERIO PRESS

Contents

About Dead End Donation

A DONATION HOLDS DEADLY secrets...

Maddie has finally found her groove as curator of the San Benedetto Paranormal Museum. The museum's fun. It's quirky. And it's all hers. But a murder and a surprise donation—an entire paranormal collection—could change the course of her small-town museum forever.

When a valuable object from the collection is stolen, Maddie suspects it may be connected to the murder of a local PhD student. Will this creeptastic collection be more trouble than it's worth? Maddie's friends and family have all sorts of ideas to expand the museum—whether she wants to or not. And as the body count rises, she must race against time to catch a killer.

If you love witty heroines, twisty mysteries, and a touch of the paranormal, you'll love this hilarious whodunit. Get cozy with this puzzling mystery now!

Praise for The Perfectly Proper Paranormal Museum Mysteries:

"Well-drawn characters and tantalizing wine talk help balance the quirky aspects of this paranormal mystery."—Publishers Weekly

Copyright

Book Cover by Dar Albert

Illustrations licensed via DepositPhotos.com

misterio press / paperback edition July, 2023

ISBN-13: 978-1-944767-98-3

Visit the author website to sign up for updates on upcoming books and fun, free stuff: KirstenWeiss.com

chapter one

THERE ARE MYRIAD BENEFITS to owning a paranormal museum.

I can take EMF meters home to check how much radiation I'm getting from my microwave. I can sleep in, since the museum doesn't open until ten AM. And I can work in jeans and a t-shirt.

Tonight was an exception.

Shifting my weight on the mansion's marble floor, I tugged up the V-neck of my little black dress. It had been ages since I'd had to break out something halfway sophisticated. Tonight I was in a cocktail dress five years out of style and a little baggy in the hips and chest. Which I guess beat the alternative.

I touched the back of my brown hair, done up in a chignon. Comfortable chatter flowed through the crowd of small-town sophisticates. Across the high-ceilinged room, my mother, chic in a sequined white dress, shot me the stink eye. I adjusted my V-neck higher.

"Better watch it," a man rumbled warningly. "I'm keeping an eye on you, Maddie Kosloski."

"Only one eye?" I turned and smiled.

My boyfriend, Jason Slate, grinned rakishly back, his brown eyes, flecked with gold, gleaming. He looked outstanding in his charcoal suit. But he always looked outstanding, even in his more utilitarian detective-wear.

I laid a hand on his muscular arm. "I didn't think you were coming."

As I'd hoped, he edged closer. I had to angle my head upward to meet his gaze. Catching the scent of his spicy cologne, my heart beat faster.

"The chief wanted me to represent the PD's mud-run team," Jason said.

"*You're* running?" Shame on me for griping about my mother roping the museum into being one of the run's sponsors. At least I didn't have to dig out my jogging shoes. They hadn't seen any action since I'd bought them two years back—an overly optimistic New Year's purchase.

In fairness, they'd been on sale.

He laughed. "Not a chance. I'm just representing the department tonight."

"I take it the chief had better things to do than mingle?"

"Maybe so, but he wasn't going to tell a lowly detective his excuse." Jason glanced around the swank affair.

People in suits and dresses drank champagne and made small talk beneath the private mansion's glittering chandeliers. Faux-Greek columns, their Corinthian capitals shimmering with gilt, made a show of holding up the white-painted walls. Guests carefully avoided sitting on the antique, white and gold furniture. The atmosphere was elegant and oppressive—a nouveau riche mausoleum.

We were in San Benedetto's version of the White House. I'd have felt more at ease in the *actual* White House. The Secret Service had nothing on my mother.

She eyed me beadily from beside a hovering waiter. Palms damp, I turned the champagne flute in my hand.

"Why is your mother looking at you like that?" Jason asked, twin lines appearing between his dark brows.

"Maybe she thinks if she stares hard enough, I won't spill anything on the carpet."

He choked back a laugh. Fear of spillage and sinking necklines aside, I was enjoying being a medium-sized fish in the small pond of San Benedetto.

It had taken me a while to get used to it, especially since my mother was constantly bragging about my more successful siblings. But I liked my small-town life. I had a great boyfriend, wonderful friends, and a fun and fulfilling job. I couldn't imagine changing a thing.

Jason bent his head closer. "Where do you think our hostess is?" His breath tickled my neck, and I shivered.

My mother materialized at his side. "Preparing for her grand entrance." She nodded toward the balcony at the top of the stairs. "Nell always did have flare." She turned to Jason with a gleeful smile. "Has Maddie told you? Her sister Melanie's decided to get married at her fiancé's villa in Sicily."

I bit back a groan. My siblings were big fish in rarified international ponds. I was trying not to feel insecure about my comedown from my previous, high-flying international career. Or at least not to *act* insecure.

A balding man in a rumpled blue suit slouched toward us. Relieved by the potential interruption, I waved. "Clayton?" He owned a local auto parts store, which put him in the mid-upper echelons of our social scene.

Clayton Clarke straightened his shoulders. "Maddie, I'm glad you're here."

"Why?" I blurted. My face heated. "I mean, it's good to see you too."

I'd last seen him at the police station. His father, a paranormal collector, had died under suspicious circumstances. And then a woman had been killed at his father's estate auction. And while the murders had been resolved, none of it had been easy on Clayton.

The effect of murder on the survivors was different than of a loved one's natural death, or even of an accident. Murder was evil, and evil left a mark.

Clayton's brows drew together. "There's something I should—"

A glass clinked. We looked toward the sound.

A fit, white-haired woman in a silvery dress and pearls stood upon the interior balcony with a raised champagne glass. "Welcome to my gala honoring our Mud Run sponsors. Proceeds from the run will benefit the San Benedetto Historical Association." Our hostess, Nell Grandall, motioned to an older woman in the crowd below.

Harriet, director of the Historical Association, smiled up at Mrs. Grandall and awkwardly adjusted her ruby-red dress. She looked like she felt even more out of place than me.

"Change is inevitable," Mrs. Grandall continued.

I bit back a sigh. California was changing at a record pace, and I was sick of it. I was sick of the growing buildings, blotting out the sky. I was sick of the thickening traffic. I was sick of seeing the past bulldozed for a soulless vision of the future. But there wasn't a thing I could do about it.

"Nevertheless," the older woman continued with a nod to the woman in red, "we are products of our past. The San Benedetto Historical Association is helping to preserve that past. Understanding our history helps us understand how our current town came to be and how to manage the changes. When my ancestor, Vincenzo Benedetto, founded San Benedetto, he could not have imagined what it would one day become." Her mouth trembled. She blinked rapidly and coughed. "But you know why you're here. So let's get on to our surprise. Clayton?"

Clayton adjusted his glasses and climbed the curving stairs. The rest of us applauded politely.

"Of course, you all knew Clayton's father." The older woman tittered. "We were all both a little jealous and—may I say—a little worried about that lovely, haunted house of his."

Clayton grimaced, and I shot him a sympathetic smile. Unlike his eccentric father, he was no fan of the paranormal. And as a paranormal agnostic myself, I had a soft spot for skeptics.

Clayton came to stand beside Mrs. Grandall on the landing. He straightened his navy tie. "So most of you know my father had a, er, remarkable collection from the American spiritualist movement, which he kept at his house." He cleared his throat. "What, uh, I didn't know until recently, was he also had a second, private collection."

I frowned. More private than the stuff he'd kept at his house? Viewing that collection had been invitation-only, and I'd never gotten an invitation. I also hadn't been able to afford much at the estate sale. Mr. Clarke's collection had been light years out of my price range.

"I'd like the town to benefit," Clayton said. "So... Well... Why draw out the suspense? I'm donating the entire collection to the San Benedetto Paranormal Museum."

I gaped. *What?* The paranormal...? *My* paranormal museum? More polite applause washed through the room. I raised my hands to clap as well, then paused, embarrassed. Was I clapping for myself?

I was dying for more exhibits to rotate through the museum, but I never had the money. Rotating exhibits meant repeat customers. This donation could be a game changer.

Or it could all be junk. It was unlikely Clayton's father had kept any good stuff in storage. He'd have kept it at the house, where he could gloat over his treasures.

Jason rubbed my back. "Congratulations."

"Yeah," I said faintly. "Thanks." I shook myself. It was probably just a few pieces, but that could be a good thing too. The museum was short on space. Whatever it was, this was a win.

I smiled, warmth flooding my body. Clayton had already given me one special piece from his father's collection—a *Zoltar* fortune telling machine. It was amazing he was giving us more.

"How nice," my mother said in a neutral tone.

I shot her a sharp look. Had she known about this? As co-president of Ladies Aid, our local charity, she had her ear to all the important San Benedetto doings.

Not that my museum qualified as important. The real tourist attractions in San Benedetto were the wineries and the annual Christmas cow display.

Granted, the straw cow usually went up in flames every year, moving my museum up in the pecking order. People took bets on whether it would survive each holiday season. Still, being lower ranked than a giant cow stung my pride.

Clayton descended the curving staircase. Mrs. Grandall made a few more remarks which I didn't really pay attention to. I was too busy mentally rearranging my museum for the new exhibits.

Clayton made his way to me through the crowd.

"Clayton," I said, grasping his hand. "This is so thoughtful. Thank you."

"Uh..." He ran his hand over his thinning hair. "You're welcome. But it's a little more complicated than you might expect."

"How so?" my mother asked.

"There's quite a bit to go through," he said. "Perhaps we could meet at my father's storage facility tomorrow? Say ten o'clock?"

I nodded. "Sure, if that's convenient for you." Because it was also convenient for me. Tomorrow was Monday. The museum would be closed, and I could take the time to check out the donation.

Though I suspected Clayton was trying to pawn off a bunch of junk. Not that I was offended. The better part of my exhibits were junk. But sorting through it all could be a project.

I might be able to talk Herb, a paranormal collector who found artifacts for the museum, into helping. *For a price.* I gnawed my bottom lip. Herb wouldn't be happy I'd scored an exhibit or two without him.

"Excellent," Clayton said. "I'll text you the address." He strode into the crowd.

"Why do you look worried?" Jason asked me.

"An inherent lack of faith in human nature," I said. "I'd better call Herb." I nodded toward the open French doors to a porch.

"Good thinking," my mother said. "He'll be hurt if you don't. But I'd like to come tomorrow too, if you don't mind."

I refrained from comment. Where my mother was concerned, it didn't really matter if I minded or not.

"I'll meet you back here." Jason kissed my cheek.

"PDAs while on duty?" I teased. "What's gotten into you?" I strolled outside.

A couple murmured in one corner of the wide porch. I moved around the corner of the Victorian to a more private spot. Setting my champagne glass on the wooden railing, I called Herb.

"This might be Herb Linden's voicemail," he said. "Or it might not. Leave a message and find out." BEEP.

"Hi, Herb. This is Maddie. Clayton Clarke found a few more of his father's paranormal objects and wants to give them to the museum. I thought you might be interested in checking them out with me. I'll—"

BEEP.

Text you the address, I completed silently. But Herb had gotten the gist of it. If he was interested, he'd call. I dropped my phone into my black clutch. And though Jason was waiting inside, I lingered on the porch.

The April night was warm, the breeze a caress on my bare arms. I stood there for a few moments, enjoying the fresh air and solitude.

Oaks stood like gnarled sentries on the lawn inside the circular drive-way. No cars were so crass as to clutter the gravel drive. Mrs. Grandall had hired a valet service for the night. They hadn't thought much of my old pickup.

A female figure in jeans and a t-shirt hurried from the house carrying a plastic toolkit. She crossed beneath a grouping of spot-lit oak trees, a backpack slung over her shoulder. Long, auburn hair cascaded down her back and glinted in the lights from the house.

I squinted, bracing my hands on the white porch rail. "Belle?" I called out.

The woman glanced over her shoulder. It *was* Belle, my ex-boyfriend's fiancée. I waved.

She turned and hurried across the dark expanse of lawn. Belle vanished beneath an oak.

My mouth compressed. I'd thought we were on better terms than that. My relationship with Mason was far in the rear view mirror. Besides, Belle and Mason were getting married in a month.

But maybe Belle hadn't meant to diss me. The porch wasn't well lit. It was possible she hadn't recognized me.

Grabbing my champagne flute, I returned to the party inside. My mother stood beside a potted fern and spoke to Jason, her expression animated.

My boyfriend looked a little cornered, and I repressed a smile. I hoped she wasn't bending his ear about my sister's plans for an Italian wedding. He might think she was hinting at something.

I strode through the crowd to rescue him. "I don't know if Herb will make it," I told my mother. "But I'll text you the address when I—"

A woman's scream split the air, and I started, slopping champagne over the sides of my glass and onto the thick white carpet. The flow of conversation splashed to a halt.

Mrs. Grandall staggered onto the mezzanine and clutched the white railing. "Dead," she gasped. "He's dead."

chapter two

MRS. GRANDALL SAGGED ON the balcony. A muscular, youngish man in a tux rushed forward. He caught her before she could fall.

"Stay here," Jason said, terse. He raced through the murmuring crowd and up the wide, curving stairs.

My mother shot me a speculative look. She touched her throat.

"What?" I folded my arms.

"Nothing. I'm just glad *you* didn't find a body this time. I love your community involvement, but it starts to get repetitious."

"I—" I clamped my mouth shut. I wasn't sure what my defense would have been anyway. In the past I *had* found more than my share of corpses. Worried, I rubbed my face and wondered who had died.

Jason said something to the young man and to Mrs. Grandall, who seemed to have recovered herself. Jason nodded. Striding across the balcony, he disappeared down a hallway.

"I hope it's no one we know," my mother said in a low tone.

"Yes," I said dryly. "Let's hope it's someone no one knew and who was universally disliked."

She frowned. "I'd rather not have any more tragedies. Though of course the death is going to be a tragedy for *someone*."

My hands curled inward, my chest constricting. And I was being a jerk. Of course no one wanted to get bad news. Why would my mother? "Do you know many of the people here?"

"I practically know them all." She bit her bottom lip.

Jason emerged on the landing. "I'd like to ask you all to stay until an officer can take your statement. And please, don't talk to each other."

The buzz in the high-ceilinged room increased, everyone ignoring the latter request. Jason led Mrs. Grandall and the young man away.

My stomach plummeted. "It must be a suspicious death," I said. "Or he wouldn't need statements."

"Oh, dear," my mother said.

It took fifteen minutes for the first police officers to arrive. They separated us, asked us if we'd been upstairs, and asked if we'd noticed Chadwick Keegan.

Since I didn't know who Chadwick Keegan was, I replied *no* to all the above. We gave our names, contact info, and arrival times at the party to the police, and then we left.

I met my mother outside. A red-coated valet hopped from her Lincoln SUV and handed her the key. He trotted back to the house.

"Who's Chadwick Keegan?" I asked.

The moon dipped behind a cloud. A nearby oak tree creaked in the breeze.

"I have no idea." Parallel lines creased the space between her brows. "I really thought I knew everyone here. He mustn't be from San Benedetto."

"Kosloski," a woman barked.

My shoulders shot to my ears. I knew that voice.

A woman of Amazonian proportions and with closely cropped blond hair stalked toward us. "I should have known you'd be here," Detective Laurel Hammer barked. My childhood nemesis wore a fitted, navy pantsuit. It hugged every sleek muscle, no doubt built up over hours in a boxing gym pummeling my imaginary face.

"The museum's sponsoring the Mud Run," I bleated. "It's not my fault." Wait. That made no sense. But between a suspicious death, a surprise donation, and now a run-in with Laurel, I was feeling frazzled.

"What's your connection to Keegan?" the detective asked.

"Nothing. None," I said. "I don't even know who he is."

"Who *was* he?" My mother angled her head.

Ignoring the question, Laurel glared down at me. "I'm not putting up with any interference from you." Her blue eyes blazed.

"I'm not interfering," I said. "I'm leaving."

"I'm not Slate," the detective said. "He may cut you slack, but I'm not going to."

Sheesh. How many times did I have to say I wasn't involved? "Honestly," I said. "I don't know anything. I'm not doing anything. I'm going."

Laurel stepped closer. "Don't bother with the denials. You'll never change. No one ever changes."

My mother cleared her throat.

Laurel glanced at her, swallowed, and edged away from the car. "I'm watching you." She strode into the massive white Victorian.

"Thanks for the moral support," I said. Not even Laurel wanted to get crossways of Ladies Aid. They were not only the biggest gossips in town, they were also the hidden power behind whatever throne existed at town hall.

"She's not entirely wrong about you interfering. Not that I'm criticizing," my mother said hurriedly. "I believe in doing your civic duty. It's not your fault your main talent lies in solving murders."

"There's also the whole paranormal museum thing," I said, wry.

I'd turned a sleepy little sideshow into a relatively successful tourist attraction. I might be agnostic on the paranormal, but I did enjoy coming up with new marketing schemes for the museum.

"Oh," she said. "Right. You're quite capable when it comes to promotion. Text me the address for tomorrow." She climbed into her SUV.

I watched her back away. Gravel crunching beneath her tires, my mother turned the big car. She cruised down the long drive.

Suddenly exhausted, I walked to the valet stand and handed over my ticket. A few minutes later, a uniformed valet trundled up in my old pickup.

The red truck looked wildly out of place amidst the BMWs and other luxury cars lining up at the portico. But at least my truck got points for being vintage.

Unsettled, I drove home. A man had been murdered while I'd been swilling champagne and noshing on stuffed mushrooms. No one had heard and no one had known—except for his killer.

And if I double checked that the doors and windows of my garage apartment were locked, well, that wasn't paranoia or anything. It was just good sense.

San Benedetto Man Found Dead at Mud Run Fundraising Event
—San Benedetto, CA
Police are investigating after someone found a man dead and bleeding from a head injury at the Mud Run donor thank you event.

Officers responded around 7:15 PM to the home of Mrs. Nell Grandall, hostess of the event. They found Chadwick Keegan in an upstairs hall-way. Because the cause of the man's injuries were unknown, the homicide detective on the scene, Detective Jason Slate, decided investigators would conduct a suspicious death investigation.

The body was discovered by Mrs. Grandall not long after the announce-ment that Mr. Clayton Clarke would be donating the remainder of his father's sizable spiritualist collection to the San Benedetto Paranormal Museum.

Mud Run volunteers manager and Director of the San Benedetto His-torical Association, Harriet Jones, said, "It's a horrible tragedy. We knew Chadwick well at the Historical Association. He was a lovely young man." Proceeds from the Mud Run will go to the San Benedetto Historical Associ-ation.

Police ask anyone who saw anything or has any information to contact Detective Jason Slate at the San Benedetto Police Department.

I braced my elbows on the museum's front counter and studied the newspaper spread before me. The article included a portrait of a smiling Chadwick. He was dark haired and looked about my age, mid-thirties. Instead of making him look nerdy, his glasses gave him a dashing air. He was handsome. And dead.

A black paw stretched across the page.

I grunted, pulling the newspaper sideways. Tarot decks and Paranormal Museum t-shirts and hoodies flashed beneath the glass. "Not now, GD."

The paw stealthily withdrew. GD stands for ghost detecting, and the cat is a museum favorite. He had staring at nothing and looking mysterious down to a hard science. But when he didn't have an audience, he harassed me.

I tapped my fingers on the newspaper. So Mrs. Grandall herself had discovered the body. And Harriet from the Historical Association had known the victim. Should I make a condolence call, or would that seem too much like I was snooping?

Because I was most definitely *not* snooping. Not with Jason running the investigation. He could do just fine without me, and my interference would only annoy him.

The ebony cat growled. I peered over the counter at his near-empty bowl of kibble. "You've still got some left. Don't be greedy."

His growl rose to a wail that raised the hairs on the back of my neck. "Fine. One treat." Fishing beneath the antique cash register, I extracted a kitty treat. I tossed it to the checkerboard floor.

The black cat dropped from the counter and sniffed at the treat, his tail lashing. Shooting me a baleful look, he strolled past shelves lined with paranormal knickknacks. He sprang into the haunted rocking chair in the corner and coiled on its seat. Above him, haunted photos of murderers gazed down, impassive.

"Mondays," I muttered. Mostly I loved them, because the museum was closed. GD hated them *and* Tuesdays for the same reason. Like I said, he preferred an attentive audience.

Someone rapped on the front door's glass pane, and I swiveled on my high stool. My best friends, Adele Nakamoto and Harper Caldarelli, waved from the sidewalk.

Sliding from my seat, I walked around the counter and opened the door. The bell above it jangled.

"Oh my God." Adele strode inside, her pink tulip skirt swishing about her knees. She hugged me and managed not to get a black hair out of place in her elegant chignon. "That poor man. And you were there!"

"I should have been there." Harper furrowed her brow and tugged down the hem of her chocolatey knit top. A man on the sidewalk outside glanced through the slowly closing door, and he stumbled. And yes, Harper's movement and his near fall *was* cause and effect. Though Harper was of Italian descent, she looked like the actress Penelope Cruz, all curves and thick, brown hair. "But there was an emergency town council meeting—"

"It's fine," I said. "I mean, it wasn't fine. It's terrible for the man's family. And for poor Mrs. Grandall too. She nearly fainted." It had been a charmingly old-fashioned reaction. But Mrs. Grandall was old-school.

The door shut, the bell above it jingling. On the haunted rocking chair, GD sneezed.

"I read she found the body." Adele's brown eyes widened with sympathy. "And you got some sort of big donation?"

"I don't know how big it is," I rested an elbow on the brass cash register. "You remember Clayton Clarke? I guess his father had a secret stash of paranormal artifacts. It's likely all or mostly all junk. But beggars can't be choosers."

"How's he going to get a tax deduction if you're not a 501c3?" Harper asked.

"A what now?" Adele said.

"That's the California designation for a non-profit," Harper said. "I'm assuming Clayton wants a deduction."

I shifted my weight, my sneakers squeaking on the checkerboard floor. Would Clayton rescind his offer once he realized the museum was for-profit? It was a meager profit, but still, a profit. "Like I said, it's probably not worth much."

Adele checked her watch. "I have to get back to the tearoom. Let's talk more about this later." She strode to the bookshelf in the wall and pressed a spine. The bookshelf swiveled open, and she walked through it into the Fox and Fennel.

I smiled. The secret door between our businesses never got old. The bookcase swung silently shut.

"If you need any help with this donation," Harper said. "I can pitch in."

And Harper would, even though my friend was running her own financial planning business *and* working as a town councilor. "Honestly," I said, "it's no big deal. But if I need help, I know who to call."

She hesitated. "This murder... I see Jason's in charge?"

"Yeah, he happened to be at the party last night."

"And that's, er, not going to cause any problems?"

"Why would it?" I asked, bland. "He's a cop. He's in charge of the investigation."

She raised a dark brow.

"And I'm not involved," I said, resigned.

BANG, BANG, BANG.

Harper and I started. Fist raised, Herb Linden, my paranormal collector, scowled through the front window. The little man's wispy brown hair was scraped across his head.

"Hold your horses," I told him and opened the door. "Did you get my mess—"

"How dare you," Herb hissed. His coke-bottle glasses glinted beneath the museum's overhead lights.

"How dare I what?" I asked, bemused.

His jaw jutted forward. "You've ruined my *life*."

chapter three

I RAISED A BROW. "You can't be serious."

Under normal circumstances, being accused of ruining a life is something I wouldn't have taken lying down. But this was Herb, and when the paranormal was involved, he tended toward melodrama. He was just upset I'd landed a paranormal collection without his help.

Harper leaned one hip against the museum's glass counter. Her full lips quivered suspiciously. GD sat up in the haunted rocking chair, setting it swaying. The bronzed skull grinned from its pedestal.

Herb straightened his striped bow tie. "You've killed my career. And I'm your exclusive collector. We had a deal." He jerked down the hem of his tweed jacket.

We did *not* have a deal. It was more of a one-sided understanding. "I did no such thing," I said, indignant.

"You're chiseling me out of work by acquiring that secret collection," Herb said. "How am I supposed to collect for the museum, when you've got the biggest and best collection in the bag? Why didn't you tell me Clayton was donating it to you?"

"Because I didn't know until last night. And I don't know how big or best it is either."

"A likely story." He scowled. "What's in it?"

"I have no idea," I said. "Which is why I called you after Clayton told me. Didn't you get my message?"

"You know I never check messages." Behind his thick glasses, his eyes narrowed with cunning. "Where is this collection?"

"I'm waiting for Clayton to text me the address."

He sniffed. "You don't trust me with the location?"

Well, no, because that would just be dumb. Herb had nearly gotten me killed last year withholding information in a murder investigation. I liked Herb, but I didn't completely trust him. Not when paranormal objects were involved.

"I was hoping you'd come with me to view the collection," I said. "I'll need your expertise to evaluate whether I want it or not."

He lowered his head and studied me over his spectacles. "You don't want it? Clayton's father was California's biggest collector of spiritualist and paranormal artifacts. Why wouldn't you want it?"

"Because Clayton probably sold off the best stuff at that auction last year," I said.

He rolled his eyes. "This is so typical. I offer you the deal of a life-time—Dion Fortune's scrying mirror. She was the most famous female occultist of the twentieth century. And you turn your nose up at it. And now you're offered pieces from the Clarke collection—"

"I'll leave you two to it." Harper straightened off the counter. "See you around, Maddie." She walked out the door, and the bell jangled behind her.

"That mirror's still available," he said.

"No. Thank you." I couldn't afford that mirror. And it was more than a little weird that Herb was having such a hard time unloading it. Not that I was suspicious or anything.

Herb rubbed his narrow chin. "All right. I'll help you. For my usual fee."

"Naturally," I said, tone flat. I didn't expect any friends and family discounts just because I'd once nearly died on his account.

The front door opened. Mason Hjelm, the owner of the motorcycle shop next door, walked inside. He wore a black motorcycle tee and jeans, and his longish blond hair was pulled back in a short ponytail.

I smiled. We'd dated for a while, before Belle and Jason had come into our respective lives. I hadn't admitted it to anyone, but I still felt a sentimental pang at the sight of him.

Mason stopped short. His mouth pursed. "You're busy."

"Not really," I said. "It's my day off."

Herb folded his arms over his rumpled tweed jacket. "What's *he* doing here?"

"Gosh," I said. "That *is* a mystery." Which I was sure would be revealed in time.

"I saw you were in and thought I'd drop by," Mason said. "We're having an event on Friday at the shop." He angled his head toward the museum gallery and his motorcycle shop on the other side of it. "I didn't want it to be a surprise."

"Thanks for letting me know," I said. "We don't have anything happening at the museum that night. There shouldn't be a battle for street parking."

"Cool." Mason glanced down at Herb. "I heard you were at the party last night."

"No." Herb glared at me. "I wasn't invited."

I rolled my eyes. As if I'd had anything to do with the invitations. "Yes," I said. "I was. What was Belle doing there?"

"She was doing Mrs. Grandall's hair," Mason said distractedly. "What happened?"

"The murder you mean?" I asked. "Didn't Belle—?" Oh, *right*. She'd left before the body had been discovered. "I only know what I read in the paper. I didn't see anything."

"But you saw Belle," Mason said carefully.

"Yes, as she was leaving. We didn't get to talk. Why?"

"No reason." Mason backed out the door. "I'll, uh, see you around."

Herb's jaw set. "Well?"

"Well, what?" I asked.

"Well, where's this collection?"

"I told you," I said, exasperated. "I don't know. Clayton hasn't texted me yet."

"When's he going to text you?"

"Soon, I hope. We're supposed to meet at ten."

Herb stalked to the haunted rocking chair, picked up GD, and sat. "I'll wait."

"Fine." I kept myself busy checking our online orders and packing boxes of EMF detectors and Tarot decks. So Mondays were only my day off in theory. When you owned your own business, there was always work to do. And that was okay by me.

True, running a paranormal museum wasn't as high powered a career as my brother's. He worked for the State Department. And it definitely wasn't as glamorous as my sister's, who was an opera singer.

But I'd found my own quirky niche. And while the museum kept me busy, it wasn't exactly stressful work. I'd fallen into a groove, and I liked it.

My cell phone rang on the counter, and I checked the number. *Clayton.*

Herb sprang from the rocking chair so fast its back banged against the wall. "Is that him?" He set down the cat.

I answered the phone. "Hi, this is Maddie."

Herb hurried to the counter. "Is it Clayton?" he whispered.

"Good Lord," Clayton said. "What a thing to happen last night. Did you see anything? I didn't even know the poor man."

"No," I said. "I didn't know him either. And I didn't see anything. Did you?"

"Who is it?" Herb bounced on his toes.

I clapped my hand to the receiver. "It's Clayton. Calm down."

"No," Clayton said, "and I'm glad I didn't."

I could understand that. After the mess last year at his father's estate auction, Clayton had probably had his fill of police.

"Are you ready to see the collection?" he continued.

"More than ready," I said. "Mind if I bring my paranormal collector?"

"The more the better," he said in a grateful tone. "The thought of being alone with all that... Ugh."

I grimaced. I couldn't imagine growing up in a creepy Gothic mansion stuffed with paranormal junk. And I *liked* paranormal junk. But Clayton's neurosis was my gain.

"I'm ready," I said. "What's the address?"

He rattled it off. I scribbled the address onto a notepad on the counter. Herb peered at my writing, his lips moving silently.

"Great," I said. "We'll be there shortly."

Clayton and I disconnected. I turned to Herb. "Ready to see the collection?"

Herb rubbed his thin hands together. "I was born ready."

chapter four

IN THE BRICK ALLEY behind the museum, Herb started his yellow VW Bug. I opened the door to my pickup and glanced up at a curtained window.

My neighbors, Mason and Belle, lived in the apartment over my museum with their son, Jordan. I hadn't received an invitation to their wedding, but I hadn't expected one.

My phone rang in the rear pocket of my jeans. I pulled it free and checked the number. *My mother.*

"Hi—"

"Madelyn, this is your mother."

I hung my head. *Every time.* She announced herself *every* time. "Hi, Mom. I'm just on my way to see Clayton's collection."

"His father's, you mean. Text me the address. I'll meet you there." She hung up.

I didn't exactly need my mother coming along for the ride. And I wasn't sure why she even wanted to. But since I'd promised, I texted her the address and started my pickup.

I cruised beneath the adobe arch marking the end of San Benedetto's downtown and zipped down a grid of roads. The vineyards glistened emerald with dew, and mustard flowers bloomed between the grapevines.

Aprils were near perfect in San Benedetto, and today was no exception. The morning was in the high sixties. The sky was clear and blue. We'd hit seventy-something by the afternoon, and I was determined to enjoy it. Summers were miserably hot, with the added hell of quasi-tropical humidity scented with cow manure.

I didn't catch up to Herb until we'd reached the parking lot of a two-story, corrugated metal warehouse surrounded by vineyards. Pulling into a spot, I double checked the address. This was the place, all right.

Clayton, in a tan sports jacket and khaki slacks, straightened off the warehouse's metal door. He walked to my pickup and smoothed his graying hair.

I hurriedly slid from the cab. "Hi. My mom's on her way."

Herb's Bug backfired, sputtered, and died. My paranormal collector stepped from the tiny car, his chin high, and joined us. He stuck out his hand. "Pleasure to finally meet you. I knew your father."

I gave Herb a sharp glance. My understanding was he and Clayton's father had been rivals, and not friendly ones.

But Clayton merely traded grips with Herb. "You're the paranormal collector?"

Herb rocked on the heels of his loafers. "That's me." He whipped out a simple white card and handed it to him. "Maddie brought me along as an *expert* assessor." His smile was smug.

Clayton glanced at the card and shuddered. "I don't know how you can stand this stuff, either of you."

"Oh," I said, "I don't know. I think the paranormal's kind of fun."

Herb glared. "Fun? The paranormal is serious business. Clayton's father understood that. You *know* what can happen when an object isn't properly bound. I don't understand how you can *still* be so—"

My mother's Lincoln SUV purred to a stop beside us. Herb clamped his mouth shut.

She climbed from the car and adjusted her big leather purse over the shoulder of her denim blouse. "Morning, everyone. Are we all set?" she called, brushing off her white jeans.

"Some of us more than others," Herb muttered, glancing my way.

"It looks that way," Clayton said glumly. He took a deep breath, turned toward the warehouse, and squared his shoulders. "Let's get this over with." He strode to the door, hesitated, then wrenched it open and walked inside.

Herb trotted after him.

My mother raised an eyebrow. "Was I imagining it, or was Herb looking at you like you'd just run over his dog?"

I sighed. "You weren't imagining it. He thinks I've skunked him out of a major paranormal find." We followed the two men inside and into a long, dimly lit aisle.

The warehouse consisted of rows of stalls walled with chicken wire attached to two-by-fours. Stacked boxes and pieces of furniture filled the carrels. "I didn't know there was a storage rental place out here," I said to my mother. "Did you?"

She shook her head, her squash blossom earrings swinging. "It's probably less expensive than those bigger self-storage places."

Clayton stopped in the middle of the aisle and turned to face us.

"Which one is your father's?" I asked him.

"Um," he said, "all of them."

I stumbled to a halt, my brain's circuitry overloading. "All of which ones?"

"All of them." Clayton motioned down the long aisle. A line of overhead lights grew smaller in the distance. "The whole warehouse belongs to him."

I gaped. "But... That's..." What? "All of it?"

"There's so much," Herb whispered. "It's going to wreck the paranormal economy for decades."

"I know," Clayton said in a miserable tone. "It reminds me of the warehouse scene from the end of that movie. You know? The one with that adventurer archaeologist?"

"Maddie Kosloski and the Temple of Dumb?" Herb suggested.

My mother frowned.

"No," Clayton said. "I don't think that was it."

My jaw firmed. In Herb's eyes, the size of the donation had just cemented my betrayal. "Oh, come off it, Herb. I had no idea there'd be so much... of this." I motioned around the high-ceilinged warehouse. A pigeon fluttered in its metal rafters.

"The good news," Clayton said, "is my father owned the warehouse outright. So the building's included in the donation."

Aghast, I stared. I couldn't fit all this stuff in the museum. Not when I could fit a dozen paranormal museums inside the warehouse itself. Even if I had rotating exhibitions, there was no way I could manage it all.

Despite the cool air, sweat beaded my forehead. "Clayton... This is—"

"I suppose Maddie will need to create a 501c3 to accept the donation," my mother said briskly.

"It's the only way I'll get the tax deduction." Clayton pulled an unlocked padlock off one of the wire cages. "And I believe several of the pieces are quite valuable. Take a look."

My pulse pounded in my ears. *Five-oh-one ...?* How did my mother know about those?

Herb and my mother walked inside the cage. "Good heavens," my mother said. "Is that—?"

"It is," Herb breathed.

I just stood there, my arms loose at my sides. There was no point following them inside. It was too much. I couldn't handle all this stuff.

Clayton gave me a pitying look. "Believe me, I know the feeling."

"I'm not sure you do," I croaked.

My mother entered the aisle carrying a clear glass goblet. A thin blue straw curled inside it. "Maddie! It's the Benedetto Goblet."

Sure. Right. The Benedetto Goblet. Whatever *that* was. "The what?"

She raised the goblet higher with both hands. "When the Benedettos founded San Benedetto, Vincenzo Benedetto drank from this very cup to celebrate his first grape harvest. The cup came all the way from Italy. Drinking from it was said to guarantee the next harvest would be strong. I had no idea your father had such an important piece of local history, Clayton."

"If it was cursed, haunted, or lucky, my dad had it." He hugged himself, rumpling his sport jacket.

"It's San Benedetto's version of the Holy Grail." My mother held the glass to an overhead light to admire it. "Look at the detail. There are actually little grapes on the stem. Just think what other treasures might be in here. I need to call Ladies Aid." She handed Clayton the goblet and strode outside.

"I'm afraid it's all like that," he said. "My father kept his best pieces here."

"Why?" I asked. "He had that huge house."

"So he could gloat over them in secret, I suppose. It was so secret, I didn't even know he *had* this place until a few weeks ago." Clayton walked into the cage and replaced the cup. "My father was probably worried other collectors might find out about his better pieces. He lived in fear someone would make off with one of his treasures." His nose wrinkled.

I scrubbed a hand across my face. This was impossible. Amazing, but impossible. "Clayton... I hate to say it, but this is too much. I don't think I can accept it."

"Too late," Herb said from inside the cage. "Now Ladies Aid knows about the find. Do you really think they'll let this collection get broken up and go to an outsider?"

I spluttered. "But... I mean... How do you know it's *all* like the goblet? Look at this place." I motioned skyward.

Gently, Clayton took my arm. "It will be all right."

He led me to an enclosed office and sat me behind a handsome antique desk. Walking to a wine cabinet, he pulled out a bottle and uncorked it. He poured each of us a glass of something red and tossed his back. "I doubt the *wine* is haunted."

And even though it was before noon, I took a gulp. The wine was really good. Clayton's father might have had an odd taste in collections, but he knew his vino.

"I hate to say it," Clayton continued in a low voice, "but a collection of this size will put San Benedetto on the map. I *could* donate it to the Historical Association. They're a non-profit. But then there will be two paranormal collections in San Benedetto. I'm afraid your museum will come out the poorer."

I slumped in my chair. He was right. My pokey but charming little museum couldn't compete.

Sure, we might get some paranormal overflow. But the more likely scenario would be my museum getting run out of business. "So if it stays in San Benedetto with someone else, I'm screwed. And if it goes, San Benedetto is screwed."

"I considered burning the place down for the insurance, but I didn't think I'd get away with it."

The heavy warehouse door opened, and sunlight knifed into the gloom. Clayton and I glanced at each other. Wordlessly, we walked into the hallway.

My young assistant from the museum, Leo, and my mother's co-president at Ladies Aid, Cora, gawked at the cages.

Cora noticed us, shook herself, and wafted toward us, her palm-print caftan billowing. She wore a velvet tiger-print headband around her silver hair, pulled into a loose bun. "Goodness. Is this really all the museum's now?"

"We're gonna need a bigger museum." Leo unzipped his black motorcycle jacket and tilted his head backward. A shock of near-black hair slipped from over his eye.

"We're still trying to work that out," I said, trying not to hyperventilate.

"I wonder if Adele would sell her tearoom?" Cora mused. "You could expand laterally."

"I couldn't ask her to do that," I said, startled. Besides, Adele owned the whole building. If anyone was moving, it would have to be me.

The thought sent a pang through my gut. I *loved* the secret passage to her tearoom, the Fox and Fennel. Plus, they had amazing sandwiches. "What are you doing here?" I asked them.

"Oh," Cora said vaguely. "Your mother called me."

"And I was with Cora," Leo said. "Since it's museum business, I thought I'd come along. You don't mind, do you?"

"No." I clawed a hand through my hair. "I'm just not sure—"

The metal door swung open, and we winced. Light silhouetted a broad shouldered, masculine figure. Jason, in a navy suit, walked inside. He whistled. "Damn. You're going to need a new museum."

I hurried to him. "What are you doing here? Is there a problem?"

"No." He smiled down at me. "No problem. Your mother called and thought I should come."

I sucked in a breath. Who *else* had she called? And why did Jason need to come? Not that I didn't love seeing him. But this was museum business.

"What are you going to do with all this?" he asked.

"I don't know. It's way too much for my museum." I raked my hands over my scalp. "I guess I could pick out the best pieces."

"They're *all* the best pieces." Herb's voice floated to us from the depths of the warehouse.

Jason peered down the hallway. "Is that Herb?"

"He's around here somewhere." I motioned toward an industrial overhead light. My hand moved in an awkward, jerky motion.

My mother returned inside the warehouse, and the door clanged shut behind her. "I've called an emergency meeting of Ladies Aid. Obviously, you'll need help, and since this affects the town, we'll provide it. Harper can help you organize the museum as a non-profit."

"Thanks," I said, my breath quickening. I tugged at the collar of my paranormal museum hoodie. "But—"

"The question," Cora said, "is will you have a separate, non-profit museum in addition to the existing museum? Or do you turn your existing museum into a non-profit?"

"She'll need to consult a lawyer who specializes in such things," my mother said. "I'm sure Harper will be able to recommend one."

"If she can't," Cora said, "someone at Ladies Aid will have a contact. But what about the space?"

I tugged on the collar of my hoodie. Why was it so hot in here? "I don't—"

"Madelyn will simply have to get financing," my mother said. "I'm sure there's some sort of small business loan available."

"But if she's a non-profit," Cora asked, "will she qualify?"

"You're right," my mother said. "I wasn't thinking. We'll have to hold a fundraiser."

I blinked rapidly. *Fundraiser?*

"It won't be easy, coming so soon on the heels of the Mud Run," Cora said. "All the big donors have already opened their pockets for the Historical Association."

"We won't know the timing until we can get the non-profit museum organized," my mom said. "This will take some planning, Madelyn."

I swayed, lightheaded. My heartbeat pounded in my ears.

Jason grasped my arm. "I need to talk to Maddie privately. Will you excuse us?" He steered me toward the front door.

"What?" I asked. What now? Because if any more surprises were in my immediate future, my skull might explode.

"We need to talk."

chapter five

DRAGGING MY HEELS, I tugged on the strings of my hoodie as he opened the warehouse door for me. Nothing, and I mean *nothing* good ever comes when your boyfriend says you need to talk.

"What's wrong?" I stepped into the parking lot and blinked in the morning light. "Why do we need to talk?" Wasn't it enough my museum life was getting turned upside down? Was I getting dumped too?

"We don't," Jason said. "I just thought you needed a breather."

"Oh." Laughing shakily, I leaned against him, my head resting on the lapel of his suit jacket. I inhaled his twin scents of spicy cologne and authority and relaxed. "Thanks."

"You okay?"

A train clattered past in the distance. I glanced toward the far-off tracks. A water tower rose above the vineyards. We weren't far from the vineyard Adele's family owned.

"I'll be okay once I remind everyone it's my museum," I said. "I get to decide what to do."

I'd forgotten that for a moment myself. But was it really just *my* museum? It did have an impact on the community. A small, weird impact, but an impact.

And if I did decide to expand, so would the museum's effect on San Benedetto. So what *was* I going to do?

"You don't need to make any decisions today," he said, "do you?"

"No." I stepped away from him. "I mean, Clayton wants a decision so he can move on. But he's not going to make me decide right this minute." I didn't know Clayton that well, but he didn't strike me as the kind of man to push.

"Aren't you working today?" I asked. "How did my mom manage to drag you away from the police station?"

He smiled. "Clayton had left the party by the time the body was discovered last night, so we don't have his statement. This gives me a chance to ask him a few questions. And yes, it's an excuse to be here. But I'll take it."

"How is the, ah, case going?" I asked casually. I wasn't sticking my nose in. *Everyone* wanted to know. Besides, it's only polite to ask your boyfriend about his day.

A farm truck bumped past on a nearby dirt road. Plumes of dust billowed in its wake.

Jason arched a brow. "You know I can't discuss an ongoing investigation."

Heat washed up my chest and neck. "No, no, of course not. I meant generally. The newspaper article said Chadwick had died from a head injury. Could it have been an accident?"

He sighed. "No. That will be in the paper tomorrow. It's officially a homicide investigation now."

"Will the article mention the murder weapon?"

"No," he said repressively.

Then I wasn't going to learn what it had been. I knew Jason couldn't give me any details. He was a professional. He had to be circumspect. But it was really irritating.

"Are you feeling better?" he asked.

"Yes." Stomach rolling, I smoothed the front of my paranormal museum hoodie. "Time to face Ladies Aid."

We returned inside. Beneath an industrial light, Cora and my mother stood deep in conversation with Clayton. Something rattled inside a cage.

Leo poked his head from an open chicken-wire door. "There's a whole collection of nineteenth century spirit photography in here. Framed. It looks like they're signed by the photographer too. There's enough here for its own gallery exhibit."

My heart jumped. Spirit photography got its start in the 1860s alongside the spiritualist movement. While the early photographers were experimenting with new techniques, some unscrupulous ones realized there was an opportunity for profit. They used double exposure to superimpose ghostly images of relatives beside a recently taken image of the bereaved. With so many losses in the Civil War, people longed for comfort. They wanted assurance their beloved relatives were still well and watching.

Other photographs of the genre were more outré. Today, photos of ectoplasm issuing from those old medium's mouths were hot. An exhibit of spirit photographs would be a huge draw, and it would fit in well with my collection of spiritualist artifacts.

I pressed my lips tight. And this wasn't the time to plan an exhibit. "I've made a decision," I said loudly.

My mother, Cora, and Clayton fell silent.

"My decision is I'm not making any decisions until I know what the options are," I said. "Until then, no fundraisers or... anything."

"Of course," Clayton said. "I'm moving next month though, so you'll need to make a choice soon. I've got to dispose of this property one way or another."

What? My pulse accelerated. That wasn't fair. I needed time.

"Moving?" my mother said. "But what about your auto parts store?"

"Sold it," he said.

"To whom?" she asked. "Not to one of those big chains?"

Clayton nodded, the top of his balding head reddening. "They made me an offer I couldn't refuse."

A pained sound escaped Cora's throat. "But the charm of San Benedetto is we don't have chains."

"It's only an auto parts store," he said, apologetic. Clayton rucked up the sleeve of his sports jacket and checked his silvery watch. "I need to get going. If you don't mind, I should close up."

"Sure," I said, mouth dry. I could be professional, even if I wanted to kick something. "We'll get out of your hair. Have you got an inventory?"

"Yes, in the office files." Clayton nodded toward a larger carrel. "I'm afraid nothing's been transferred to electronic records. It's all typed on paper. But it's all there."

My stomach spasmed. "Typed? On paper?" I swallowed. "How... old-school." No computer records meant a lot more work. I really *would* need Herb. I looked around. Where *was* Herb?

Clayton walked to the open cage and slipped its padlock from the hook. Clayton stepped inside and looked around. "Where did you put the Benedetto Goblet?"

"I didn't put it anywhere," I said. "Mom, you had it."

"I gave it to Clayton," she said. "He returned it to the stall. I did see Herb go in there afterward."

"Herb?" I shouted. My voice echoed through the warehouse. A car sputtered to life outside. "That sounds like his VW." I jogged into the parking lot.

Herb's yellow Bug sped away. I pulled my cell phone from the pocket of my hoodie and called him.

He answered on the second ring. "You can't have it Maddie."

"Can't have what?" This was no time for him to play paranormal commando... Or whatever it was he was playing. "Herb, we're looking for the Benedetto goblet. Where'd you put it?"

Herb hung up. I stared at my phone. Jason came to stand by my side. "Problem?"

The Bug rounded a corner and vanished behind fields of grapevines. Aghast, I stared after the tiny car's dust trail. "I... think Herb just stole the Holy Grail."

I tried calling Herb again, but he refused to pick up. We searched the cage where the goblet had been stored, but it was gone. Herb really had taken it.

"What on earth is he going to do with it?" Cora leaned against a spirit cabinet. "He can't exactly sell the goblet. It's stolen goods."

"Madelyn," my mother said, grim. "You have to get that goblet back."

Cora's gaze flicked to Jason. Arms crossed, he studied a black and white photo of a Victorian woman with smoke-like ectoplasm issuing from her nose. "We *do* have a detective here."

"No," Clayton said. "No police. I'm done with the police. After what happened to my father..." He shuddered. "The goblet's still my property. As far as I'm concerned, it's been taken by an expert for evaluation."

"It's not just your property," my mother said. "It's an important artifact of the town's past. It belongs in a museum. Madelyn, get it back."

I heaved a sigh. "Fine." It was simpler to just do it than to argue. I knew where Herb lived, and I knew where at least one of his warehouses was. And if worse came to worst, I'd have a word with his mother. Or Ladies Aid would. *Heh heh.*

I returned to the museum, mainly because I was afraid my mother might follow me home to talk non-profits. But my mother always had a handy excuse to drop by. I rented my garage apartment from her sister.

Behind the museum's antique cash register, I called Harper and explained the situation.

GD leapt onto the counter. The ebony cat rubbed against the tip jar. Absently, I patted him, and he bit me.

"Whoa," Harper said. "So you're thinking of creating a real museum?"

I examined the white bite marks on my hand. "What do you mean *real?* I already have a real museum." I motioned toward the shelves of haunted objects, the framed photos of murderers on the walls. GD sneezed and migrated to the top of the old-fashioned cash register.

"Yeah," she said, "but... I mean, you've been pretty good about keeping it interesting. You've got all this great information up about the exhibits. But if this is as big as you say, it's going to be whole other level. Won't it?"

I braced my elbow on the brass register and gnawed my bottom lip. I *had* tried to professionalize the museum. We now had small placards beside each object describing its story. But was that enough?

I rubbed my forearms, rumpling my navy hoodie with its ghost logo. I'd basically inherited the museum, and I'd made a lot of improvements. But the truth was, I'd never really known what I was doing. I'd just bumbled along.

"Setting up a non-profit is easy," Harper said. "I can do that for you. But it sounds like you're talking expansion too. There are financial consider-ations."

I swallowed. What was I getting myself into?

Nothing. I wasn't making any decisions now. I was just exploring the options. "When can we meet?" I asked.

We set up an appointment. Stomach spiraling, I hung up. I didn't have to do this. I could just reject the donation and keep things as they were. It sounded a lot easier. Except for the part about getting run out of business by whoever did get the collection.

Someone rapped on the glass pane in the front door, and I started. On the other side of the glass, Mason lifted his hand in greeting and smiled. But his expression seemed strained.

I hurried around the counter and opened the door. "Back so soon? What's up?"

"I didn't want to say anything in front of Herb." He ran his broad hands down the thighs of his black jeans. His longish blond hair, pulled back in a ponytail, looked a little lank. "When Belle left the party last night, what did she look like?"

I wrinkled my brow. "I didn't really see her. She was leaving and I— Ah... Don't you know?"

"No," he said. "She didn't come back from the party on Sunday. I don't know where she is."

Ice spread through my midsection. *What?* "Have you told the police?"

"Of course. I made a report. They're not waiting twenty-four hours to look for her, because Jordan..." He trailed off.

I swallowed. Anabelle might abandon a fiancé, but she wouldn't aban-don their son. Not willingly. "Who'd you talk to at the police station?" I asked. "Jason might be able to help."

His Baltic gaze met mine. "Jason already knows. That's who I talked to."

My heart dropped. Jason knew. Jason had known Belle was missing.

And he hadn't told me.

chapter six

THERE ARE CERTAIN REALITIES when it comes to amateur detecting. The main one being, I was an amateur. Jason was a professional. He had to tread a fine line with information, and I got that.

I was also seriously pissed off. And that wasn't going to help anyone. I exhaled slowly to calm myself.

A muscle jumped in Mason's jaw. His hands pressed flat against the glass counter. Muscles bunched beneath his motorcycle tee.

GD dropped like liquid from the brass cash register. The cat rubbed against Mason's black boot.

And I could be mad later. I swallowed my hurt. "I'll help any way I can."

My neighbor nodded, curt. "Thanks."

"What have you done so far?"

He shook his head. "Aside from reporting it to the police, I've talked to Belle's friends at the salon. They haven't seen her."

"What about social media?"

His eyes widened slightly. "I hadn't thought of her social accounts." He pulled his phone from the rear pocket of his jeans.

I'd actually meant posting that she was missing. Her friends online could keep an eye out. But maybe Belle *had* posted something recently.

My heart sank even lower. *Could* she have just... left? But she wouldn't leave their son. And she and Mason were getting married next month.

"There." He thrust the phone into my hand.

I scrolled through the images. There were photos of the Grandall house, the Victorian lit for the party. And a picture of Mrs. Grandall, her white hair done up and smiling. But nothing after that. "Is there a way to track Belle's phone?" I asked.

"Not for me. We weren't exactly keeping tabs on each other."

"All right." I returned his phone. "I'll put the word out on social media. And I'll talk to Ladies Aid too."

He raised a blond brow. "Ladies Aid?"

"They helped find Harper last year, and they pretty much know everything that goes on in this town."

He nodded. "What else?"

"I guess we could talk to Mrs. Grandall," I said slowly. "She would have been one of the last people to see... I mean from the party," I fumbled and scrubbed a hand over my desk.

Dammit. I hadn't meant to imply Belle was dead. She couldn't be dead. "Of course, other people have seen her, we just don't know who they are yet." Oh, *that* sounded smart.

"You think Belle's disappearance is connected to the murder, too," he said, his voice thick.

"Ah... I don't... I mean, we can't assume anything." But it was an odd coincidence, Belle vanishing from a party where a man had been murdered. *Belle* couldn't have killed him, could she have?

"Great," he said. "Let's go talk to Mrs. Grandall."

"Ah... She's... I don't think she's the sort of person who likes people just showing up on her doorstep. I'll ask my mom to get us in."

He glowered and folded his arms, his muscles bulging. "We don't have a lot of time, Maddie."

"I know, but my mom will work fast. Trust me, this will be more efficient in the long run."

"Belle must have seen something." Mason dropped his arms. "And now she's on the run. It's the only thing that makes sense."

But why not run to the police? "According to the newspaper article, Harriet at the Historical Association knew the murder victim. The association should be open now. Why don't I go talk to her, see what I can learn?"

"I'll go with you."

"Okay, but talking to Harriet is a long shot. Are there places Belle liked to go? Other friends you could talk to?"

He tugged both hands through his mane of hair. "The lake. She liked the lake."

My heart squeezed. They were supposed to be getting married at the lake. "Okay. You check the lake. I'll call Ladies Aid and get something set up, and then I'll head to the Historical Association. I'll let you know what I learn."

"Thanks." He strode from the museum, the bell over the door jangling.

GD looked up at me and meowed.

"No," I said. "I don't know what's going on either."

I called my mother. Fortunately, she could be cool and efficient when the situation demanded. After an initial protestation of shock, she agreed to set up a meeting between us and Mrs. Grandall. She also promised to get the word out to Ladies Aid.

"Several of the women were—are clients of Belle's," she said. "They may be of help."

Not *were* clients. *Are* clients. My mother was working on the assumption Belle was still alive too. And for some reason, that was a comfort. "Thanks," I said. "I'm headed to the Historical Association."

"Good. Harriet knows about the goblet. She may be able to help."

"Wait, what do you mean she knows? She knows Herb has it, or she has general, useful information about it?"

"Both, of course."

"Already? How does she know Herb took it?"

"I called Herb's mother. She told me she has nothing to do with his collecting and didn't want to know. And then Cora called a few more members, asking them to keep an eye out for him. Word got around."

I sighed. "Herb's no criminal." But had he taken the goblet in a fit of paranormal-collecting revenge? "I don't know what he's up to, but we'll get it back."

"Maddie, you *have* to. You have no idea how important that goblet is to the town. I'm afraid Mrs. Grandall may have found out too. She's rather obsessive about her family history. But of course, Belle is the priority right now. Keep me informed." She hung up.

Locking up, I drove to the Historical Association, a white-painted Victorian at the edge of San Benedetto's old town. I climbed the porch steps and reached for the ornate wooden door.

As my fingers grazed the knob, the door sprang open. A fit, fifty-something redhead burst from the Victorian with a sob. I couldn't see her face—it was buried in a tissue. But her red dress looked expensive. She brushed past me and hurried down the wooden steps.

Gaze clouding, I looked after her for a moment, then walked into the cool hallway. Sunlight from the window above the door glinted off wood floors. The scent of lemon polish hung heavy in the air. To the right was a closed wooden door marked: *Office.*

I knocked.

"Rea?" The door opened, and Harriet peered out, her round face wrinkled with concern. "Oh, Maddie, it's you. I thought..."

"Was Rea the woman I just saw leaving? The redhead?"

She raised a hand to her curling white hair. "Did she leave? Poor thing. She and Chadwick were very close. They got to know each other well during his research. I'm afraid his death has hit her hard. But come in, come in. I suppose you're here for information on the goblet?" She turned and walked into the office, her khaki skirt swishing.

Rea had known the dead man? I filed that factoid away. The more people who knew him, the more who might have an inkling as to why he'd been killed. And the more who might have an idea if Belle was connected to the crime.

"That would be useful," I said, "but I don't want to intrude. I'm sorry, what research was Chadwick doing?"

"On the history of old San Benedetto of course." She sat behind an antique, wooden desk. Curlicues spiraled along its legs. "For his PhD. He was writing his dissertation on our founding father, Vincenzo Benedetto. Fascinating man. Vincenzo was forced to leave Sicily, you know, when he refused to pay the mafia's extortion. It's why he came to California. The goblet was one of the few things he brought from the old country."

"I'd have thought Vincenzo's history would have already been pretty well mined."

She shrugged. "You know how it is when you're getting a PhD these days. *Everything's* been well mined. PhD candidates have to go deep, go niche."

"Where was Chadwick getting his PhD from?"

"UC Davis." Harriet braced her elbows on the wooden desk. "It was quite convenient, since his employer was so close."

"His employer?"

"He was working part-time at the Association of California Historical Associations."

"Ah..." *Association of associations...?* "I'm sorry, the what?"

Harriet smiled, and I caught a whiff of peppermint schnapps. "It is rather a mouthful, isn't it?" she asked. "Most people just call it the ACHA, though I dislike acronyms. The San Benedetto Historical Society is a member."

ACHA? "It sounds like a sneeze."

She smiled benignly. "The ACHA meets quarterly. Lucky for us, we're close enough we can attend in person. It's given us all sorts of networking advantages."

"When's the last time you saw Chadwick?" I asked.

"Upstairs, yesterday." She pointed to the white ceiling. "He was digging through our archives that Sunday. I nearly had a heart attack when I heard him upstairs. We were closed, but Rea had let him in, so it was all right. I had no idea he'd gone to the Grandall party later."

"You didn't see him there?"

"No. His death has been such a shock. He really was a nice young man." She lowered her voice. "He came from money you know, but he was extremely hard working."

"No, I didn't know," I said, thoughtful. Money provided all sorts of motives for murder. But I needed to focus on Belle. "Do you know Belle Rodale?"

"The hairdresser?" Harriet sat back in her executive chair. "Of course. She's making quite a name for herself among the ladies of the town."

"Did you see her at Mrs. Grandall's party last night?"

"No. Was she there? Now, about the goblet." She pulled open a desk drawer. "I have a file. Normally, I would charge you for this research. But your mother explained everything." She handed me a manila folder. "Everything you need to know is in there."

"Thanks." I flipped through the file. "I can't believe you found all this for me so fast."

"Oh, that was easy. Chadwick had already pulled it all together."

My scalp prickled. I met her gaze. "*Chadwick* was researching the goblet?" Chadwick the murder victim had researched the now-stolen goblet? That Herb now had? *What the hell?*

The white-haired woman nodded. "As part of his research into Vincenzo. He found the goblet fascinating. I suppose he thought a lucky goblet would spice up his dissertation."

"If Rea was helping him, I'd love to talk to her. About the goblet," I added hastily.

"I'm not sure when she'll be back. But I'll give you her number." She thumbed through a box of business cards and wrote a number on a notepad in an elegant hand. She tore the page free and handed it to me. "Here you go. If you need anything else, let me know."

Feeling like I'd been dismissed, I muttered my thanks and left the Victorian. A limo idled on the other side of the driveway.

I opened the file folder and ambled toward my faded red pickup. A gust of wind scented with cow pasture fluttered the pages. I slapped the file shut in time to walk into a solid male body.

"Oof." I looked up and winced. "Sorry."

A blond-haired man stared down, his blue eyes cold. His muscles strained against his black sports jacket. He was tall, tanned, and muscular. The guy was big enough to have his own gravity field.

He jerked his head toward the limo. "Get in."

I swallowed. "Excuse me?" Why did he look so familiar? I'd swear I'd seen him before. But where?

"In. The limo."

"Ah... No, thank you. I've never been kidnapped before and think I'll pass on the experience."

That said, if I ever did get kidnapped, I didn't think I'd rate a limo. Besides, it was broad daylight. At the *Historical Association*. Who got kidnapped from a historical association?

He grunted and grabbed my elbow, propelling me toward the car. "The limo. Mrs. Grandall wants to talk to you."

"Hey!" Anger heated my face. *Mrs. Grandall could just—* "Augh." My feet tripped over themselves, but I kept moving forward.

Hold on. My kidnapper was the guy from last night who'd caught Mrs. Grandall from falling. "Right," I said. "Good. I want to talk to her too." So *there.*

He opened a rear door and didn't quite shove me inside. I landed on the seat with another *oof.*

Mrs. Grandall, in a powder blue tracksuit and pearls, cocked her head at me from the opposite seat. "So good of you to see me." A cut crystal decanter half-filled with an amber liquid sat inside the middle arm rest. Two matching glasses bracketed it in burnished-wood cupholders.

I laughed uneasily. "Did I have a choice?" Seriously. Did I?

"We all have choices." The old lady leaned forward. "Now, I've heard from your mother."

"Oh, good. Mason was hoping to—"

"The goblet, Ms. Kosloski. You need to retrieve that goblet. *Now.*"

chapter seven

"Ah..." I shook my head. "Sorry. What?" The limo's engine hummed discreetly. A/C blasted from the vents at my feet. The door locks clicked shut.

"Vincenzo Benedetto's glass goblet." Mrs. Grandall's voice crackled with impatience. She swung one leg over the other, missing my knee with her powder blue running shoe by a whisker.

"Don't worry," I said. "I know who has it."

"I know who has it too." Mouth pinching, she sank back against the black leather seat. "That strange little man, Herb Linden. God only knows what he'll do with it—most likely sell it to one of his strange friends. You need to get it back. It belongs to me."

I blinked. "To you?" It was horribly possible. In the past, Clayton's father had been "loose" with some of his acquisitions. It wouldn't have been the first time he'd been accused of trafficking in stolen goods.

Were the bowels of that warehouse full of jacked artifacts? My head swam at the thought.

She huffed and sat back in her seat. "Vincenzo Benedetto was my great, great, great grandfather. By rights, that goblet is mine." She smoothed the front of her track suit.

"How did Clayton's father get it?"

"How should I know? I thought the goblet had been lost, that one of my sisters had taken it when our father died. And then my *sisters* all died, and it vanished into one of their children's collections. No one would admit to having the goblet, but that would be quite typical. My nieces and nephews have no sense of heritage."

"Could one of them have sold it to Clayton's father?" *Please, don't let it be stolen.* This mess was complicated enough without adding hot goblets to the mix.

Mrs. Grandall sniffed. "It hardly matters. The point is, it's a relic of my family... and of the town's past. My ancestor founded this town. Any relic associated with him matters."

"Okay. Well. I'm working on it."

"At the Historical Association?" Her lips pressed together. "Learning the history of the goblet won't help you retrieve it."

Yeah... I couldn't argue that, so I changed the subject. "Actually, I'm glad you found me. There's something else I wanted to talk to you about." My stomach growled. Loudly. It was always quick to remind me when lunchtime was near.

"I'm afraid I don't keep snacks in my car."

My face flamed. "No, that wasn't—"

"And if you're looking for donations for your new paranormal museum, that will largely depend on whether you retrieve that goblet."

"I'm not looking for money," I said. Though maybe I should be. But that didn't matter now. "A woman disappeared from your party last night. Belle Rodale. I believe she did your hair?"

Her lipsticked mouth puckered. "What are you talking about?"

"Belle left your party and hasn't been seen since."

"So she was seen *leaving* the party?" she asked.

"Yes, I saw her leave the house." But I hadn't seen her get into her car. If the car had been abandoned at Mrs. Grandall's, Mason would have mentioned it though.

"Then I don't know what you're asking *me* for. She didn't disappear from my party. She disappeared *after* my party. What would I know about it?"

That was... *also true,* and I sank lower in my seat. Mrs. Grandall might be old, but time hadn't dulled her wits. Now I was a little embarrassed I'd suggested to Mason we talk to her.

I tried to redeem myself. "Was Belle behaving strangely when you saw her? Did she seem to be under any stress?"

"She—"

Someone rapped on the tinted window. Mrs. Grandall rolled it down.

Harriet peered inside the limo, her white hair brushing against the top of the window. "Oh, there you are, Maddie! And how lovely to see you again, Mrs. Grandall."

Mrs. Grandall inclined her head in a regal manner. "How can we help you, Harriet?"

"I thought you might be interested, Maddie. Chadwick had a brother, Price. He stopped by the Historical Association one day." Her round face crinkled with distress. "I'm afraid they argued."

"Why would Maddie be interested in that?" Mrs. Grandall asked. "How does that help her find the goblet? You don't think this Price person has it? I thought Herb Linden had absconded with the glass."

"The goblet?" Harriet's brow furrowed. "No, because of the murder. Maddie's always interested in murder, aren't you dear?" She smiled. "We all know how much you've helped the police in the past. And you've been so discreet about it, a real credit to Ladies Aid."

I wasn't a member, but I nodded anyway. "When was this?"

Harriet tapped her chin with a gnarled finger. "Oh, about two weeks ago, I'd say."

"Thanks," I said. "I'll talk to Price."

"He lives here in San Benedetto," Harriet said helpfully. "He owns the Breath Winery."

Mrs. Grandall loosed a soft laugh. "The names they'll give wineries these days."

"He's following in the footsteps of your ancestors," Harriet said. "Not the name, of course. But the wine. Did you know Vincenzo Benedetto was the first person to plant a vineyard in San Benedetto?"

"I may have read that somewhere," I said. Like in every single tourist brochure for the town.

Mrs. Grandall preened. "The original vineyard still exists, though the wine isn't sold publicly. I would have offered it at the event on Sunday, but—"

"Of course," Harriet continued loudly, "Napa has us beat. They first started growing grapes for wine in the 1700s."

Mrs. Grandall and I narrowed our eyes. Napa was lovely. But in my opinion, their wines were overpriced and overrated. Just because they had rolling hills and San Benedetto was flat as the proverbial pancake—

"I'll leave you two to your *tête-à-tête*." Harriet extracted her head from the open window. "Have a lovely Monday."

Mrs. Grandall rolled it up. "Napa," she snarled.

"The wineries there have gotten a little ridiculous," I agreed. Some charged upwards of fifty bucks for a *tasting*.

Her lips pursed again. "Well? Are you going to look for that goblet or not?"

The door beside me opened. The blond muscle man loomed outside it.

"Thank you, Thane," Mrs. Grandall said. "Ms. Kosloski was just leaving."

"You were going to tell me something about Belle," I said, planting my butt more firmly in the seat. "About whether she seemed odd or stressed that night?"

"No."

"No, you weren't going to tell me anything?"

"No, she didn't seem *stressed*, as you put it. She did my hair, and that was all."

"Does she do your hair often?" I asked.

She cocked her head. "Does it matter?"

Thane reached into the limo, grasped my upper arm, and hauled me out. It was a little rude, if you asked me.

I brushed off my Paranormal Museum hoodie with sharp, short movements. "For a chauffeur, you must get in a lot of gym time."

"I'm a personal trainer." He moved to shut the car door, but I wedged my hip into the opening.

"Hey," I said to Mrs. Grandall. "Was Chadwick's brother, Price, at your party?"

"All the Mud Run sponsors were," she said.

I backed away. Thane shut the car door and got into the driver's seat, then he closed that door as well.

The limo cruised away, kicking up dust in its wake. I coughed, waving it away with the manila folder.

Returning to my vintage pickup, I dropped the folder on the seat and texted Mason: TALKED TO MRS. GRANDALL. SHE DOESN'T KNOW ANYTHING.

I hesitated then sent another text. AND NOT TEXT SHOUTING. STUCK IN ALL CAPS.

I reread the last sentence. It seemed the story of my life.

chapter eight

MASON RAISED HIS BROWS. "You're eating a burrito?" He wove through the tiled patio. Big umbrellas sheltered the red plastic tables. "Now?"

Not yet. Resigned, I closed my mouth and set down my uneaten burrito. I was starving, and *any* time's a good time for a burrito. But I bit back my retort.

The skin beneath his blue eyes was shadowed. His black motorcycle tee had deep wrinkles, as if it hadn't been washed lately, and an ache pinched my heart.

I shoved a red plastic basket across the table at him. "Eat. I got you your favorite, the super carne asada with hot salsa and no sour cream."

Mason grunted. "Thanks." He sat in the plastic chair across from me and it sagged beneath his weight. Mason's arms didn't have the definition of Mrs. Grandall's chauffeur/personal trainer, but he worked out.

He cocked an eyebrow at me. "What?"

My face warmed. "Nothing."

He unwrapped the foil from the burrito. "What'd you find out?"

"Not much. Mrs. Grandall pointed out—rightly—that I'd seen Belle leaving her house. She has no idea what happened to her afterward. And Belle wasn't behaving strangely during the haircut. I asked Harriet from the Historical Society too. She didn't see Belle at the party at all. You?"

"She wasn't at the lake." He bit into his burrito. No bits of food dropped out. So either the carne asadas weren't as messy, or Mason had burrito-eating superpowers.

I watched, fascinated, as he took two more bites. Not even a drop of green salsa dribbled from the tortilla. "And I assume her car wasn't left at Mrs. Grandall's house?" I asked.

"No." He swallowed. "The police confirmed that. Look, Belle disappeared after a party where a man was killed."

"Actually, she left before the body was discovered," I said absently. But she might not have left before Chadwick had been killed. I didn't know when he'd died. Though if she'd seen something, why hadn't she gone to the police? It made no sense.

I picked up my burrito. A black bird with yellow eyes landed on the patio beside Mason's boot. It cocked its head hopefully.

I ripped a tiny piece off my tortilla and tossed it to the red-tiled patio. The bird snatched it up. It flapped to the low fence railing dividing the patio from the parking lot.

"There's a connection." Mason rubbed his face. "And the police think so too."

I stilled, burrito halfway to my mouth. Warmish green salsa dribbled onto one finger. "What? Why do you think that?"

"The questions Jason asked me. It was obvious he thinks her disappearance is connected to the murder. What'd you find out about this Chadwick guy?"

I returned the burrito to its basket. If I dug in now, I'd just make a huge mess like I always did. And even though Mason was a friend and only a friend, I didn't want to slop food down my hoodie in front of him.

I wiped my finger on a paper napkin. "He was working on his PhD dissertation at UC Davis and doing research for it at the Historical Association. And he had a part-time job with the Association of California Historical Associations."

"The what?"

"I know." *What a name.* "But it's really a thing. Our Historical Association is a member. Chadwick also had a brother named Price. They were heard arguing at the San Benedetto Historical Association a couple weeks ago."

He grunted. "Was Price at last night's party?"

"I think so. Apparently, he was a sponsor of the Mud Run."

He eyed me. "I saw the museum is a sponsor too. You in the race?"

I barked a laugh. "Are you kidding? Me? Run? And through mud? Only if someone was chasing me." And what were the odds of *that* happening?

Mason grinned and wadded up the aluminum. Damn, he was already finished?

"What's next?" He tossed the foil in a nearby trash bin.

"It's Monday," I said. "The ACHA is open. But if we get there before the cops do, they might accuse us of interfering with their investigation, prejudicing witnesses, that sort of thing."

Mess or no mess, I couldn't hold out any longer. I grabbed my burrito.

"Don't care." He rose and took my arm.

"Ah…" I strained to take a bite and missed.

"Let's go."

We took my pickup. I loved Mason like a brother, but there was no way I was riding all the way to Sacramento on the back of his Harley. Also, I figured I could keep my burrito warm on the dash. Its foil had to have heating properties.

The ACHA was in one of Sacramento's leafy historic neighborhoods. I parked on the sidewalk, and we climbed the concrete steps to the brick, prairie-style home.

Mason opened the green door for me. I walked inside the foyer, my feet sinking into a pale, floral-patterned rug. Elegant dark-wood stairs led up to the second floor. A potted fern stood on a narrow table beside the diamond-paned window.

Mason and I looked at each other. He shrugged, the muscles beneath his black t-shirt rippling. He walked to a partially closed door and knocked.

No one answered. He pushed open the door and leaned in, then withdrew. "No one's there," he said in a low voice.

"The door was open," I whispered. "Someone's got to be here." Unless the killer had gotten here first. But that was silly. My lungs squeezed. Why—?

Footsteps sounded upstairs. Involuntarily, we looked toward the white ceiling.

Mason climbed the first few carpeted steps. "Hello?" he called. Feeling like an intruder, I followed.

A slight, middle-aged man appeared at the top of the stairs. His thin salt-and-pepper brows lowered. "What are you doing here?" Despite his slender frame, his voice was pure bass.

"We're friends of Chadwick's," Mason said, before I could respond.

The man's narrow face pinched. "And I repeat, what are you doing here?"

"You know Chadwick was killed last night?" I asked.

"Yes," he said. "The police were here earlier, disrupting our work."

I scraped a strand of hair from my cheek. It didn't escape my notice that the man seemed more annoyed by the disruption than by the shock of a man's death. But I was relieved the police had come. Now we couldn't be accused of interfering.

At least, I hoped that was how it worked. I was still a little fuzzy on the rules.

"I'm with the San Benedetto Paranormal Museum," I said.

He snorted. "Oh yes, the big announcement about the *donation*." He put the last word in air quotes.

"I'm researching the Benedetto Goblet," I said. "My understanding was Chadwick was as well. I was hoping to get access to his research materials."

"So you aren't really friends." The man folded his arms over his tweed jacket. It actually had patches on the elbows. But I refused to believe he was a professor moonlighting at a historical association. It would be too on the nose.

"I was friends with him," Mason lied. "I suggested Maddie come here. And you are?"

The thin man stiffened. "Dr. Milford MacDuff. I'm the director."

"Were you at the party last night?" Mason asked.

"Yes," he said, "though I had no idea Chadwick was there. He didn't have an invitation. He seemed to have snuck in on ACHA coattails. It was quite irregular, and more than a little awkward when I learned of it from the police."

His murder was awkward? Or his appearance there at all? "Why would Chadwick do that?" I asked.

The director relaxed his arms at his sides. "No idea. If he'd consulted me, I would have told him not to. It was a private party."

"How long has Chadwick worked here?" I asked.

"Three years," Milford said.

"What exactly did he do?" I asked.

"Research. He was a talented amateur. Why are you asking me this? I thought you wanted his research."

"I would like to see it, if it's available," I said.

"All Chadwick's work is property of the ACHA," Milford said. "And I haven't had time to go through his office."

Then why not say that upfront? My jaw hardened.

"Have the police gone through his office?" Mason asked.

"Yes. They made a real mess of things, but at least they gave me receipts for everything they carted off."

My heart fell. So much for finding out more about the goblet. And then I remembered that hadn't been my actual goal. But why *not* find out more? It was a little weird that the murdered man was connected to one of my artifacts.

And why was I thinking of the goblet as *my* artifact? I hadn't even decided if I'd accept the donation.

"Do you recognize this woman?" Mason pulled his cell phone from the rear pocket of his black jeans and climbed higher. He extended the phone toward the man.

Milford shook his head. "No. Who is she? The police asked about her too."

My stomach gave a sickening lurch. The police had been asking about Belle? They really *did* think there might be a connection.

"She disappeared from the party where Chadwick was killed," Mason said.

"Then she likely killed him," Milford said. "Or the killer killed her too."

The back of Mason's neck corded.

Could Milford be any more insensitive? "Did Chadwick have conflicts with anyone you know of?" I asked hastily.

"No," the director said. "Why would he? He was only a part-time work-er. If he had any conflicts here, we would have fired him. And I don't see why you care, if you're really interested in his research."

Before I could think up a plausible excuse, the door behind me opened and shut again.

"Hallooo," a masculine voice called. "Milford? You here?" A rotund man with thinning gray hair appeared at the bottom of the stairs. Behind his glasses, his gray-blue eyes widened. "The Paranormal Museum lady. Are you thinking of joining the association?"

"Sorry," I said. "Do we know each other?"

"No, you don't know me. I'm Bob Bobberson. I'm on the board here. I saw you at the party. Terrible ending. Poor Mrs. Grandall. She worked so hard to make it a success."

"It wasn't so great for Chadwick either," I said.

"Even worse for him," he said cheerfully. "But I didn't know him well. The part-timers don't usually mingle much with the donors. Milford makes sure of that." He chuckled. "Don't you, Milford?"

The director's face turned a shade of puce. "Mr. Bobberson. What can I do for you today?"

"I just wanted to stop in and see how this business with the murder was affecting the ACHA."

"Chadwick's loss was a tragedy," Milford said. "But it won't affect our operations. As you said, he was only part-time."

The phone rang in the pocket of my navy hoodie. I extracted it and checked the number. *Jason.*

"Sorry," I said. "I have to take this. Would you excuse me?"

I hurried across the carpeted foyer. Brushing past Mr. Bobberson, I walked onto the concrete porch. "Jason," I said breathlessly. "What's up?"

"Did I catch you at a bad time? I thought the museum was closed today."

"It is closed. I'm in, er, Sacramento." Briefly, I closed my eyes.

"What's in Sacramento?"

I drew a deep breath and exhaled. "The Association of California Historical Associations."

There was a long silence. "What's going on, Maddie?" he asked.

"I'm helping Mason. He's worried about Belle." My chest hardened. So I guessed I was still a little angry Jason hadn't mentioned that angle to me. And yes, I *was* being unreasonable and unfair. But these were friends. At least Mason was.

"And you've found a connection between her and the ACHA?" he asked.

My teeth clenched. Jason *knew* the police were investigating as if her disappearance might be connected to the murder.

But he didn't know why we'd come here. His question was fair. I exhaled.

"Not that we know of," I said. "But Belle disappeared from that party where Chadwick was killed, and he worked here. No one here seems to know anything about her. I've put the word out that she's missing through Ladies Aid. And I've posted a request on social media for information."

Jason groaned. "Ladies Aid?"

"You know they have contacts you don't," I said sharply.

"And you know you can't interfere in a police investigation."

My pulse grew loud in my ears. "I'm looking for a missing woman, that's all."

"That isn't all, and you know it."

I leaned against a squarish column. "It's not my fault she disappeared from a party where someone was murdered." I immediately regretted my words. They'd sounded childish, pettish.

Behind me, the door opened. Mr. Bobberson nodded to me with a smile. He trotted down the concrete steps to a waiting silver Lexus with tinted windows.

"Sorry," I said shortly. "I didn't mean it that way."

Jason sighed. "I know. And I know you're trying to help a friend. But it wasn't fair of Mason to drag you into this."

"He didn't—" Why was I trying to defend Mason? He could take care of himself. "I want to help. I know Belle." We'd never actually been friends, but I thought she was a good person. And Mason loved her.

The passenger window in the Lexus rolled down. Rea, from the Historical Association, rested her elbow on the open window, her chin propped on her fist. The car rolled away.

chapter nine

I JOGGED DOWN THE ACHA stairs to the lawn. The Lexus vanished around the shady corner, and I cursed. But the odds of me catching the car had been low. A leaf blower started up at a home down the street.

"—next?" Jason was saying in my ear.

"Sorry," I said, sticking a finger in my other ear. "Can you repeat that? It's a little noisy out here."

"Where are you headed next?"

I sat on the bottom stair. The day had grown warm, but the concrete step was still cool. "I don't know. Mason's talking to the director of the ACHA. He was at the party last night, apparently." A squirrel scampered up an elm tree that shaded the house.

"Mason's there? With you?"

"Like I said, he's worried."

"Is this going to be a problem, Maddie?"

I straightened my spine. "Me? Or Mason?"

"Mason, of course. How's he holding up?"

"He's managing by taking action."

Jason exhaled slowly. "If he takes action that puts him in the middle of a police investigation, it won't help Belle, and it won't help him."

I kneaded the skin between my brows. "I hear you."

"Be careful."

"I will. I wish..." I wished we were doing this together. I wished Mason's fiancée hadn't vanished. I wished I didn't feel so damn guilty and didn't understand why I *did* feel guilty.

"There's something else you should know," he said. "Mrs. Grandall has asked the police to intervene on the matter of the goblet. She wants us to arrest Herb."

"What? It's not her goblet. She can't order an arrest." I shook my fist at the sky. *Herb, you're in over your head.*

"Which I explained to her," he said. "She wasn't happy about it though. Laurel tells me she's pretty passionate about her family history."

"Tell me something I *don't* know," I grumped and sighed. "I wish you were here."

"Can I see you tomorrow?"

"Please."

He laughed softly. "I'll take you to that steak place you like. Pick you up at six?"

The door opened behind me again, and I twisted on the stairs. Mason emerged from the house.

"It's a deal," I said. "I'm looking forward to it."

We said our goodbyes, and I hung up. Rising, I brushed off the seat of my jeans. "Anything?" I asked.

Mason shook his head. The sun glinted off his golden hair. "MacDuff didn't see or hear anything at the party. I showed him Belle's picture. He didn't recognize her."

"I'm sorry." We were running out of threads to pursue, and it disturbed me to realize I felt... relieved.

A part of me was afraid to find out what had happened to Belle. And that was cowardly. My mouth compressed. It also left Mason twisting in the wind. Some friend I was.

Mason studied the residential street. A garbage truck rumbled past. "He told me Chadwick didn't get along with his brother, Price."

Who'd also been at the party. So there *were* other leads to follow, and I couldn't be gutless about following them. "That sort of reinforces what Harriet told me about their argument. Want to talk to the brother?" The odds that he'd noticed Belle at the party were low. But maybe...

Mason nodded, but his face tightened. "Are we chasing our tails? Jordan..." He trailed off.

Jordan. When you're a kid, your world centers around your parents. I couldn't imagine what their son was going through. No, that wasn't true. I *could* imagine it, and that was worse.

A dull, gray feeling settled in my chest. "Yes. Probably. But it beats sitting at an empty museum with GD."

One corner of his mouth lifted. "So you're helping me to keep *yourself* from going stir crazy."

A knot squeezed my throat. "Why else?" Lightly, I punched his shoulder. "Come on. Let's get a drink."

We drove back toward San Benedetto and into the grid that made up its wine country. Grapevines twisted on wires, low to the ground, their emerald leaves broad.

We turned at a small wooden arrow that read *Breath Winery.* My pickup jolted down a dirt road. I glanced in the rearview mirror. A trail of dust kicked up behind my wheels.

Most of the tasting rooms in San Benedetto were converted barns or farmhouses. The Breath winery was newer and built along the lines of an Italian villa. I parked outside a high adobe-colored wall.

Mason and I walked through an arched wooden gate and into a stone courtyard. Couples lounged beside wine barrels and at wire tables shaded with green umbrellas.

The temp was a pleasant seventy-something, and the sun was shining. I inhaled the scent of fresh air and wild grasses, and a sense of calm descended on me.

We walked inside the tasting room. It was an artful, high-ceilinged affair with baroque paintings in gilt frames and more wine barrel tables. At the long, wooden bar, we asked for Price.

The bartender smiled uncertainly and flipped her long, brown ponytail over one bare shoulder. "He's just had a death in the family. I'm not sure if he's available."

"It's why we're here." I handed her my Paranormal Museum card. "We were at the party last night. And we're looking for a woman who disappeared from that party."

She hesitated, studying my card. Then she nodded and hurried from behind the bar. The bartender vanished down a shadowy hallway.

Mason braced his elbow on the bar's burnished wood. "Think telling Price why we're here is the right play?"

"He lost his brother." Or he'd *killed* his brother. Were we about to question a murderer? I swallowed, mouth dry. Maybe a drink *wasn't* such a bad idea. "And like you said, we don't have time to waste."

After a few minutes, the server returned. "Price is in his office. It's down the hall and to the right." She pointed to a paneled hallway.

"Thanks," Mason said. He strode down the hallway, and I followed him to a door with a brass placard marked OFFICE. Mason knocked once then opened the door and walked inside.

A sallow man with prominent cheekbones rose from behind a wooden desk. His brown hair was carved into dark waves thanks to a robust application of product. Gold cufflinks gleamed at the wrists of his Italian suit in tasteful charcoal. "I'm Price," he said. "How can I help you?"

"I'm very sorry for your loss," I said, and Mason nodded, curt. "And we're sorry to intrude at such a time. But it's urgent. I'm Maddie Kosloski—"

"From the paranormal museum," Price said. "I remember."

"And this is Mason Hjelm," I said.

"My staff member mentioned something about a missing woman?" Price pressed the tips of his fingers into the desk, his knuckles whitening.

"She left the party last night and hasn't been seen since." Mason pulled his phone from the back pocket of his jeans, tapped the screen, and extended it across the desk. "This is Belle. Did you see her?"

Price's gaze flicked to the phone. The man did a double take and frowned, reaching for it. He took the phone from Mason and studied the screen. "I *did* see this woman. She nearly ran me over."

"Excuse me?" I said.

"Metaphorically speaking." He handed Mason the phone. "I was leaving one of the upstairs bathrooms. She was moving so fast, she knocked into my shoulder—not even an apology. I was annoyed at the time, but you say she disappeared?"

I nodded. "I didn't realize there were upstairs bathrooms available to guests." Several downstairs bathrooms had been open to guests. Belle must have been upstairs doing Mrs. Grandall's hair. But what had Price been doing up there, where his brother had been killed?

Price smoothed his striped tie. "I know the house well and figured there'd be a traffic jam downstairs, so I went up."

"You're friends with Mrs. Grandall?" I asked.

"Did she say anything to you?" Mason asked.

Price shot me an uncertain look. "Your friend, you mean? No. Like I said, not even an apology."

"Did you see anything unusual last night?" I asked.

"Aside from your friend, no. I did tell the police about her. Anyone who was upstairs..." He trailed off and swallowed.

I stiffened. Jason had known about this encounter, and he hadn't mentioned it to me either. Maybe he'd felt he didn't have to. Maybe he figured I'd get the information myself, and this way he wouldn't be violating any rules.

And I needed to get over myself. This was his investigation, not mine. And amateur detectives had to accept the crumbs they were thrown.

"The way she was moving, she seemed upset," Price continued. His jaw hardened. "I thought... Well, I thought she might have had something to do with my brother's death."

"She didn't," Mason said shortly.

"Did you ever see Belle in your brother's company?" I asked.

Price shrugged, and the lines of his elegant suit didn't budge. "No. My brother had his own life," he said, his voice tightening. "And I have mine."

"Was he involved in the winery?" I motioned about the elegant office.

"No. Chadwick wasn't big on real work. Not for the family. He had his own interests."

I studied the man. His fingers bowed more deeply as they pressed against the desk. I was pretty sure I hadn't imagined the rancor in his voice. "I didn't realize this winery was a family business."

"Was. Past tense. My father started it. He died two years ago and left it to us both. Not that Chadwick cared," Price said bitterly. "Though that doesn't matter now. Not anymore." Blinking, he looked toward a paned window overlooking a vineyard.

"Did you see anyone else around?" Mason asked. "When you saw Belle, I mean."

"No," he said. "We were alone in the hallway. No one was chasing her, if that's what you're asking."

Mason jammed the phone into his rear pocket. "Thanks." He strode from the office.

Hurriedly, I dug a business card from my wallet and slid it across the polished desk. "If you think of anything, will you let us know?"

He stared at the card. "Yes. Yes, I think I will."

I hesitated. "Was Chadwick your guest at last night's party?"

"No. Why?"

"The ACHA said he hadn't been there as a representative of the organization. I'm just curious why he was there."

Price frowned. "I don't know. Until I ran into him, I had no idea he *would* be."

"You *saw* your brother at the party?" I asked, trying to ignore the excitement bubbling in my chest. Were we about to actually learn something useful?

"In passing." Price's brow pinched. "He was too busy to talk."

"Why do you think he *was* at the party last night?"

"I assumed Mrs. Grandall had invited him. She's passionate about local history, particularly history connected to her family." His brow wrinkled. "Though he wasn't dressed for the party. He looked like he'd just come from work."

"Why do you say that?"

"He had his laptop bag over his shoulder. What does this have to do with your missing woman?"

"Maybe nothing. It's just... strange. What happened to your brother, and then Belle disappearing from the same party. I thought there might be a connection."

"If you figure it out, let me know."

I nodded, and left, thoughtful. My brother and sister were in far-off Europe, busy with their lives. We didn't see each other often, or even talk as often as I'd like.

But we loved each other. And if one of them died suddenly, I'd be a lot more broken up about it than Price had appeared to be. I cut a glance at the office door.

Mason waited for me in the tasting room. In silence, we walked onto the brick patio. A guitarist set up his equipment beside an ivy-covered wall.

Mason rubbed the back of his neck. "Belle saw something. She saw something, and she was scared."

"We can't be sure of that," I said, uneasy.

"She was upset," he said tightly. "You heard him."

Belle could have been upset about something else. But if she had seen something, if she had been running... My chest tightened. She could have been running from a killer.

chapter ten

TOUCH GRASS HAD BECOME an incredibly irritating saying. It was especially irritating when a nearby mower was blowing up my hay fever. I sneezed.

"Gesundheit." Harper hammered a yellow arrow sign into a tree beside the dirt trail running along the lake. Morning mist rose from its glassy surface. Earth moving equipment roared in the distance, yellow, dirt crusted machines scraping the ground to create the massive track. "You okay?"

On the opposite side of the trail, I unwound the *Mud Run* signs, strung between strips of yellow plastic. I stretched a sign between two trees and glanced at the cloudy sky. "I'm okay. I'm just worried. Belle's still missing."

And it was Tuesday. She'd been gone more than twenty-four hours. And the longer she was gone, the lower the odds...

Harper turned to me and rucked up the sleeves of her coffee-colored athletic jacket. "You, Ladies Aid, and the police are looking for her." Her brown eyes were serious. "If Belle wants to be found, she'll be found."

And that was the crux of it. Did Belle want to be found? Or was it impossible for her to want anything, because she was dead?

Don't go there. I coughed, clearing my throat. "Won't the rain damage these signs?"

"No." Harper's full lips curled upward. "Besides, we're counting on rain to make the race conditions worse." Her expression turned serious. "And you can count on me to help you figure out the organizational structure of your new museum. I know it's not just Belle and Mason that've been keeping you so quiet this morning."

My insides bottomed. *That donation. Expansion.* Where was I going to expand *to*? And how? "There's a lot to figure out before I get to organizational structure."

"You've got this. We'll create a non-profit, you'll find a new location, and boom. The town's got a real tourist attraction."

"The paranormal museum *is* a real tourist attraction," I said crossly. We were the third biggest attraction in San Benedetto. Second biggest, in the months the giant straw Christmas Cow wasn't up. "The museum gets tourists."

She canted her head. "You know what I mean."

Alas, I did. My museum, as quirky and charming as it was, was small and cluttered. "But I *like* being next to the tearoom."

Harper studied the trail. "Adele's tearoom's been doing well. She may want to expand."

"Into the museum?" My hand spasmed, crushing one of the plastic-y signs. Adele owned the entire building. Technically, she could do what she wanted. But I knew Adele wouldn't push me out. She was too kind.

And that was the problem. She'd never ask me to leave.

I grimaced. Adele would find a new location for the Fox and Fennel tearoom before giving me the boot. And that wasn't right.

Harper shrugged. "I'm just saying. This may be a win-win for everyone."

"Yeah," I said gloomily. "Win-win." I knew I was supposed to be adult and businesslike about the museum. It was a *business*, after all. My business. And while I loved tinkering with it—adding new promotions and events was my happy place—this seemed like a really big tinker.

Worse, it felt like the expansion was being forced on me. So my instinctual response was to dig in my heels and resist. The fact that this was also the immature response didn't change my reaction.

We moved down the trail, adding more signs for the runners. It was a high-risk event, and waivers were required, but we didn't want runners getting lost.

Harper and I rounded a bend to an obstacle that had already been set up. It was a z-shaped climbing wall that bridged a pit.

A group of raucous youths—somewhere between boys and teens—blasted water into the pit from a nearby tanker truck. Harper frowned. "It's too soon for the water. The run isn't until the weekend."

I sighed. "I don't think they're volunteers." I raised my voice. "Hey!" I strode toward the group.

They noticed me, dropped the giant hose, and scattered into the woods. The canvas hose flopped around, gushing water and trapping one of the boys beside the water truck. The boy hopped over the flailing hose, slipped in a puddle, and fell into the rapidly filling pit.

Since the pit was only a foot deep, I wasn't worried about drowning. But I reached in anyway and yanked him upright by the collar of his t-shirt.

He came up sputtering and wiped his eyes. Harper turned a crank on the truck, cutting off the flow of water, and the hose went limp on the muddy ground. The boy blinked, his blue eyes startling against his muddy face.

"Jordan?" Releasing him, I stepped backward. I wiped my wet hand on my *Paranormal Museum* hoodie. My gut lurched. I'd have to tell Mason about this, and I *hated* being a narc.

The pre-teen shook his head, spattering my jeans with mud. "Hey, Maddie."

"You know you're not supposed to be fooling with the equipment."

He cocked his head. "Do I though?"

My mouth compressed. Kids these days were a lot smart-assier than they had been when I'd been young. I blamed the internet.

"And why aren't you wearing a jacket?" I winced. *And cut your hair, and get off my lawn, and kids these days.* I sounded like my mother.

I shifted, uneasy. His attitude was too easy-breezy for someone whose mother had gone missing. "Do your parents know you're here?" I hedged.

"My mom's out of town."

Out of town? A weight flattened my lungs.

Mason hadn't told him.

And I guessed I couldn't blame him for putting it off. Mason was probably hoping Belle would return before he had to tell Jordan. "Your *dad's* not out of town," I said severely, "and it's a school day. What are you doing here?"

"It's a half day," he corrected. "Teacher conferences."

Great. "Well, stay away from the Mud Run. It's not safe."

He shrugged and trotted into the underbrush after his friends.

"Why do I get the feeling he's not taking my warning to heart?" I muttered.

Harper laughed. "Because you've got two eyes and a brain?"

I turned. "That's—" My foot slipped sideways.

Harper grabbed my arm before I could fall. I straightened, shifting my weight gingerly. Sure I was just wearing jeans and my usual paranormal museum gear. But I didn't want to have to drive home covered in muck.

I let a slow breath escape me. "That was—" My feet skidded from under me. Harper whooped, and we were both flat on our backs in the mud.

I stared at the gray sky. The ground beneath me squelched. "It's an omen," I said, "isn't it? We're cursed."

Harper sat up and looked around. "Come on. We've got more signs to put up, and it's not that bad."

It *was* that bad. Mud had gotten down my back and slithered unpleasantly against my skin. But I finished putting up the signs and hoped the mud would dry before I had to get into my truck. I knew it had dried when I started to itch.

I drove home, cleaned up, and researched non-profits online. And when Jason picked me up for dinner that night, I was waiting and dressed in a green knit top, high boots, and a skirt.

I sipped a Zinfandel and studied my full plate. We sat on the chop house's deck, overlooking a slow-moving creek.

"Was the Mud Run setup that bad?" Jason asked.

I smiled and laid my hand atop his. "Sorry. Everything's just piling on at once. Belle. Mason. The museum..."

"Have you figured out what you're going to do with the new exhibits?"

I don't *think* I made a face. I tried hard not to. But it figured he'd pick *that* subject to latch onto.

"No," I said. "Harper promised to help me sort out the non-profit issue tomorrow. She says it's not that hard. But that's only part of the problem. The bottom line is I need a new museum. I *could* rotate exhibits. But it would be a lot of work, and I'm not sure I'd get enough people inside my tiny museum to justify the cost."

"What about the warehouse?" Jason sliced into his rib-eye. "Isn't that included in the donation?"

"You mean... turn the warehouse itself into a museum?" It wasn't a bad idea. The space was large enough. I could do something modern and industrial. Or sci-fi creeptastic. But both options would take money I didn't have. On the other hand, so did buying a new space. Maybe I could lease...?

"How's Mason holding up?" he asked.

I shook my head. "I haven't seen him today. But I did run into Jordan. He seems to think his mother is on a business trip."

Jason grimaced. "Poor kid. I hope he never has to learn the truth. But as time passes, the odds are getting lower."

"Jason—"

"What did you find out?"

I exhaled. "Nothing that you didn't, I'm sure. We talked to Price—Chadwick's brother. The way he talked about Belle, like she was upset, running... You don't think she could have seen something related to the murder?"

He set his steak knife on his plate. "It's possible. But why not come straight to us?"

"You don't think the killer intercepted her before she had a chance?" I asked carefully.

"We're keeping a lookout for her car."

It wasn't an answer. Or it *was* an answer, but one I didn't want to parse too finely. I studied my plate.

"What else did Price tell you?" Jason asked.

"He said he saw his brother at the party, laptop bag over his shoulder, but—"

"Laptop bag?"

"Yes." I straightened in the high-backed chair. "You didn't find the bag with Chadwick's body?"

"No," he said. "We haven't found a laptop—not at Chadwick's office or home. You're sure that's what Price said? He saw his brother with a laptop?"

"With the bag," I corrected. But it would be logical to presume a laptop would be inside.

Thunder rumbled, and we glanced across the field. Dark clouds massed in the east.

"Looks like the Mud Run's going to be a hit," Jason said lightly.

I nodded, smiling at the change of subject. But the subject hadn't changed. Not for me.

chapter eleven

"Look," Harper said, "it's really simple..."

When you hear that, you know what will follow is *never* going to be simple. Stuffing down my frustration, I sank lower in my chair and settled in for a lecture.

Waitresses whizzed past us in the tearoom. Oblivious, my friend expounded on boards of directors, registration forms, and tax exemption requests. I munched an apricot scone and felt my eyes glaze.

"She's going into a fugue state again." Adele snapped a pair of long fingers in front of my nose.

I blinked. "No, no. I'm listening. Bylaws. Yeah."

"I can handle the paperwork," Harper breezed on. "In fact, why don't you just put me on your board?"

"Would that be a conflict of interest?" Adele asked. "What with you being a town councilor and all?"

Harper drummed her fingers on the white tablecloth. "Good question. I'll look into it."

"Of course you'll have to upgrade," Adele told me.

"You mean, move?" I'd been dreading this conversation. But I had to face facts. Adele needed more space, and the museum was in the way.

"No," she said. "I meant an audio tour, treating the collection like what it is—a real museum collection. Or even having guided tours."

I swallowed. I'd need to hire more people. I didn't have the *money* to hire more people. But I had to stop thinking like that. If the museum became a nonprofit, I could fundraise.

Fundraising. My forehead grew damp. I *hated* begging for money. It was the main reason I'd become a Mud Run sponsor instead of a runner. Runners were expected to find sponsors of their own.

At a nearby table, a gaggle of women laughed loudly. I fiddled with my napkin.

And if I had more staff... I'd need a bigger museum. I groaned and braced my head in my hands. "It's no use pretending. I'm going to have to move."

"Don't worry about me," Adele said. "You know I only wanted the museum here because downtown needed the attraction."

I raised my head. "And now it will lose it. There's nowhere else downtown I can put the museum. This inheritance is a curse."

"You don't know that," Harper said in an irritatingly reasonable tone. "I'm sure we'll find a place to put the museum. If not downtown, then we'll find somewhere nearby."

"What about turning Clayton's warehouse into the museum?" I asked.

"It's too far away," Adele said. "We need something closer."

"She's right," Harper said. "It's a bad location."

"The whole town's in a bad location," I said, exasperated.

Central California had been left out of the natural beauty lottery. Sure, it was nice enough, with its old barns and vineyards. But we didn't have the mountains, or the ocean, or even Napa's rolling hills. And it got hellishly hot in summer.

"That's not true," Harper said. "Rural and out-of-the-way have become selling points in the new, over-crowded California. San Benedetto's wonderful."

I shot her a knowing look. Harper *had* to say that. She was on the town council.

But that didn't make it untrue. I'd even come to think of San Benedetto less as a place of banishment and more as a cozy haven.

I rose and set my napkin on the table. "I have to get back to the museum."

"Hold on." Adele hurried from the table. She returned a few minutes later with a white paper bag. "For Leo."

"Thanks." I slouched to the bookcase and pressed a spine. The case swiveled open, and I strolled into the museum.

Since it was a Wednesday, only a few customers wandered the aisles. They squinted at placards and wanded exhibits with the EMF devices the museum provided.

Our new EMF detectors had been inspired by a paranormal museum in Deland, Florida. They seemed to be a hit. I'd probably need to buy more for the new, expanded museum. Assuming our visitor count expanded too.

But would we get more visitors? What if we didn't? What if I expanded and no one came? My stomach burned.

Leo looked up from behind the glass counter and shoved his shock of near-black hair out of his eyes. "That for me?" He looked hopefully at the bag I carried.

Beside the tip jar on the counter, GD's green eyes narrowed, tracking the bag.

"From Adele." I set it on the counter.

GD looked away. His black tail flicked.

"Thanks. I'm starving." The rumble of Leo's stomach was only slightly muffled by the black leather jacket he wore. He pulled a wrapped sandwich from the bag. "Did you sort out the new museum?"

I rubbed my forehead. *Oh, sure.* I just waved my magic wand and voilà, new museum sorted. "Not really."

GD butted his head against Leo's hand.

He laughed. "Don't look so depressed. The museum's growing. It's a good thing."

I forced a smile. "Of course it is."

"Did Herb bring that goblet back yet?"

"No." But I knew where my paranormal collector lived, and my jaw hardened. "I'm going out to his place to get it now. Do you mind watching things here?"

"Nope. It's my job." He bit into his sandwich.

I walked toward the door. It opened as I reached for the knob. Rea, the weeping woman I'd seen at the Historical Association and then later at the ACHA, walked into the museum.

Her red hair glittered with moisture from the fog outside. It dampened the shoulders of her trench coat, belted at the waist. A stylish black purse was slung over her shoulder.

The woman stopped short. "I'm looking for Maddie Kosloski?" She looked to be in her mid-fifties. Fine lines spoked from the corners of her brown eyes.

"That's me," I said, taken aback. Her appearance at two places Chadwick had been connected to, her emotional outburst, had all made me curious about the woman. The fact that she'd just strolled in off the street seemed too good to be true.

"I'm Rea. Rea Bobberson." She stuck out her hand, and we shook.

"Not related to Robert Bobberson?" I asked.

"He's my husband," she said, brisk. "May we talk? I was at the party Sunday night."

Make that three places. "Ah, yes." I looked around. "This way."

I led her into the Fortune Telling room, which as I'd hoped, was empty. At the round seance table, done up in bright sixties colors, I scraped back a chair. I motioned Rea to the other seat. "What can I do for you?"

She drew a shuddering breath. "You have something of a reputation in San Benedetto."

"Oh?" I asked, wary. "You're not in Ladies Aid, are you?" I was already tracking down the goblet for them. And for me. But that was beside the point. If they'd already found another errand for me, they could just get in line.

"No," she said. "Why?"

My shoulders relaxed. "Nothing. Just curious."

"I've been told you're someone to go to when one would rather not go to the police."

The muscles between my shoulder blades stiffened. "What idiot told you that? Why would anyone want to talk to a paranormal museum curator instead of the police?"

Her mouth pursed. "You... They said..."

"Sorry." Why was I chasing her off? If she had anything interesting to say, I'd just tell Jason. "But why don't you want to talk to the police?"

She twisted her fingers on the table. "It's about Chadwick. I think I know why he was killed. I think he knew something he shouldn't have."

I studied Rea. Her coppery gaze, steady and serious, held mine. It was the look of an honest person, forthright and direct. But I didn't trust it and didn't believe her.

Why come to me? Why not go to the cops? It made as much sense as Belle's inexplicable disappearance. Rea was here for another reason. To find out what Jason knew?

But because of Belle—because of the pain of that disappearance to Jordan—I asked, "What was that?"

Rea shook her head. "Is it true you were responsible for bringing down the last mayor?"

"Not really. He pretty much brought himself down." I was still a little embarrassed by how *not* involved in that imbroglio I'd been.

Her face fell. "But you *have* been involved in helping the police, right? I need your assurance that this is confidential."

So she *did* know I was connected to Jason. She was here because she wanted intel. Little did she know I had none to give.

I sat back in the wooden chair. "I can't do that. If you have information about a crime, you should tell the police. And if you give me information about a crime, I have to give that to the police too. What did Chadwick know that got him killed?"

Rea grimaced. Pushing back her chair, she stood. "Of course, you're right. I *should* talk to the police. Thank you."

I blinked. That was it?

But apparently it was, because she walked from the room. I followed her to the front door, expecting her to turn and ask me something else. But she didn't.

Uneasy, I watched her pace down the brick sidewalk. Rea had said she should talk to the police. But would she?

I called Jason. And because this was the kind of luck I was having, it went to voicemail.

"Hey," I said, "Rea Bobberson stopped by asking about the murder. She didn't tell me anything, but... I think she might know something." I hesitated. "Anyway, I just wanted to tell you. Bye." I disconnected.

Shaking my head, I walked to my pickup, parked in the rear alley, and drove to Herb's house. My paranormal collector lived with his mother in a neat Victorian sandwiched between two vineyards. A goat grazed between the vines.

Herb's yellow VW Bug was notably absent from the driveway. But I walked up the fading porch steps anyway and knocked.

After a moment or two, a white-haired lady in loose jeans and tennis shoes opened the door. "I thought you'd be by." With her free hand, Mrs. Linden adjusted the green crocheted shawl over her shoulders. She leaned on a cane with the other.

"Herb borrowed a goblet from me—"

She sniffed. "He stole it, you mean. Ladies Aid has been giving me an earful about that goblet. And no, I don't know where my son is, and I don't know where that goblet is either."

"Oh," I said, deflating.

"Have you tried calling him?"

"Multiple times. He's not answering."

Mrs. Linden pulled a cell phone from the pocket of her jeans. "He'll answer me." She dialed and pressed the phone to her ear. "Herb? Someone's here to talk to you." She handed me the phone.

"I need that goblet, Herb," I said.

"My mother?" he hissed. "You're harassing my mother now?"

"I'm not harassing her," I said, irate. I glanced at Mrs. Linden, and she frowned. "I came to see you, and she answered the door." It wasn't my fault he was still living with his mother. But women who live in their aunt's garage apartments shouldn't throw stones. "Now where's my goblet?"

"*Your* goblet?" he asked. "So you *have* decided to accept the donation."

My hand tightened on the phone. "What's going on? You're no thief, so I haven't ratted you out to the cops. Yet. Why steal the goblet?"

"You don't understand what you've gotten yourself into. It's dangerous."

Mrs. Linden's mouth compressed. She stepped backward from the door and edged a bit to the side.

"Then please," I said. "Explain it to me. Is the goblet connected to Chadwick's murder?"

"What? No!"

"Then why's it dangerous?"

"Stay out of this. I'll take care of everything." He hung up.

"Dammit," I muttered. I glanced again at Mrs. Linden, half hidden behind the door frame. "Sorry. I guess you heard that." I extended the phone to her.

Instead of taking it, she pulled a shotgun from behind the door.

Hastily, I raised my hands. "I was just kidding about calling the cops. I don't know what's going on with Herb, but I'm sure he's got a good reason for taking the goblet."

"Step aside," she said in a hard voice and looked past me.

I stepped aside and glanced over my shoulder.

The trainer, Thane, glared down.

chapter twelve

"THIS IS PRIVATE PROPERTY." Mrs. Linden held the shotgun steady. Its dark barrel gleamed dully. The day dimmed, the sun ducking behind a cloud and casting the Victorian in shades of gray.

Meanwhile, I'd seemingly hardened into a block of petrified wood, emphasis on *petrified*. I'd seen her use that shotgun before. This should have been a comfort. The old lady hit what she aimed at, and she wasn't aiming at me.

But one of the selling points of shotguns is they have a wide spread. Even though the barrel was aimed at Mrs. Grandall's musclebound minion, I wasn't sure I was in the clear.

Also, let's face it, pulling a gun on every rando who turns up at your front porch seemed an extreme reaction. I'd always considered Herb delightfully quirky. I was starting to wonder if his mom had veered into not-so-delightfully nuts.

Thane seemed to have been immobilized as well. No expression flickered across his tanned face. His blue-gray gaze did not flick toward the gun aimed at the gold, center button on his chauffeur's jacket.

I smiled weakly. "Hi, Thane." *Just act like everything's normal. Maybe her finger* won't *twitch on the trigger.* Which, if memory served, she'd once told me was a hair trigger. *Gulp.* "What are you doing here?"

The goat bleated in the yard and shook his horned head. The bell around his neck jingled.

"Mrs. Grandall wanted to know about the Benedetto Goblet," Thane said, ignoring the old woman in the doorway.

Dismissing her as a threat cemented my impression he wasn't very bright. In the history of bad reactions, disregarding an outraged woman with a shotgun was only a short step up from mansplaining to one.

"Have you found it?" he continued.

"Er," I said. "No. Not yet."

"Does she have it?" He inclined his head toward Mrs. Linden.

"No," she growled. "I don't. Now get off my porch."

"Mrs. Grandall wants to see you," he said to me. "Three o'clock." He pivoted and walked down the steps, the porch shivering beneath his weight. Thane paced the driveway to the black limo, waiting at the end.

Mrs. Linden lowered the shotgun, and I sagged. My future might not exactly be bright, but at least I had one again.

"Stupid woman," she muttered. "She's already called me three times about that goblet."

"Who?" I asked, surprised. "Mrs. Grandall?"

"She's obsessed. Your mother only called once," Mrs. Linden said pointedly.

Oh, boy. "Sorry about that."

"He's going to see a shaman."

"What?"

"Not what. Who. Herb's going to see a shaman." She banged the end of the shotgun on the wood floor, and I started. "If you hurry, you can catch him there. Fellow out in Lodi."

"Lodi. Got it. Thanks." Legs watery, I hurried to my pickup. My visits to this house never went well. I made a mental note to remember that in the future.

There weren't a whole lot of shamans in Lodi, at least not that I knew of. But Herb had once used a shaman from Lodi to de-curse some haunted cowbells for me. (Long story). It had to be the same guy. And if it wasn't...

Well, I *did* have better things to do at the museum. But Leo was there, and Wednesdays were never all that busy. I could take the time for a short road trip.

Window down, I drove down flat rural highways. The vineyards were thick with green grass and yellow mustard flowers.

The breeze streamed across my skin, and the joy of just being alive swelled in my chest. Being on the wrong end of a shotgun, even one not aimed at you, enhances your appreciation for life's small pleasures. But it didn't take long for my in-the-present euphoria to give way to monkey mind.

At what point had I gone all-in on my paranormal museum? When had it stopped being an embarrassment? Stopped being something I'd been railroaded into after I'd been fired from my more lucrative, exciting, and international career?

I'd distracted myself from that fall from grace by focusing on building the museum. And at some point, the museum had become more than a placeholder job. It had become more than a stopover while I waited to restart my "real" career.

I'd come to take... *pride* in the paranormal museum. And I guess being its curator had become part of my identity. Which was a little weird, since I still wasn't entirely sure I believed in the paranormal. But pride was the only reason I could come up with to explain my resistance to all the proposed changes.

My museum wasn't exactly prestigious, but an expansion might put it on the map. And I found I really didn't care about the museum becoming a big deal. Or at least a bigger deal. A year ago, I might have. But not anymore.

So what if my sister was an opera singer, bouncing around Europe and swilling champagne with counts? Or if my brother spent his evenings at cocktail parties with foreign diplomats? I got to spend my afternoon hunting down a shaman and a paranormal collector with a stolen goblet. My work was *fun.*

The shaman lived in a modern, pale blue townhouse with a thick, manicured lawn. I didn't see Herb's yellow VW on the street. But knowing Herb, he'd parked it down the block to avoid any cops he might imagine were on his tail.

I hurried up the paving stone walk and knocked on the black-painted front door. A hummingbird sampled a geranium spilling from the nearby window box. It tried a few more reddish-orange flowers, found them wanting, and zipped away.

After a moment or two, a cadaverous man with a salt-and-pepper goatee frowned down at me. "Yes?" He intoned.

"Xavier? It's me, Maddie. From the paranormal museum."

He broke into a crypt-keeper smile. "Ah, yes. Are those cursed cowbells giving you any more trouble?"

"No. Thanks. Ah, is Herb here?"

"You just missed him."

I cursed, and he lifted a brow. "Sorry," I said, face warming. I was trying not to swear so much. The museum got a surprising amount of young visitors. "It's just that he took this goblet—"

"The Benedetto Goblet? Yes, he asked me to bind it, but the curse on that one is even stronger than the one on those bells. I told him we'd need at bare minimum another binding box, and those are not easy to find."

"Cursed? I thought it was lucky, providing a good harvest and all that?"

He shrugged his narrow shoulders. "Perhaps it was at one time. But not anymore."

"What sort of curse?" It seemed like the sort of thing a sophisticated paranormal museum owner should ask.

"I can't be entirely certain. But given the dark energy around it, I'd say it involved some sort of blood magic."

I felt the blood drain from my face and puddle somewhere around my bellybutton. "Blood...? Magic? You mean—?"

"Murder."

It took approximately a half second to reject the idea that the goblet was connected to Chadwick's murder. And not because I didn't believe in curses. Because I sort of did.

But the goblet had been locked up in that warehouse until Herb had liberated it. Also, the goblet was old. If there *was* a curse attached to it, odds were whatever bad thing had happened, had happened long ago.

Even so, I confess the idea of a curse unnerved me. I couldn't stop turning the idea over in my head as I drove back to San Benedetto.

I was zipping through the vineyards when my cell phone rang. Normally, I'd ignore it until I got somewhere I could take the call. But I thought it might be Mason with news of Belle, so I pulled over and answered. "Hello?"

"Hey," Leo said. "We're out of maps."

I grimaced. Since the museum had been included in the visitor's map, we were obligated to keep maps on hand for our guests. "I'm not far from the Wine and Visitor's Bureau. I'll stop in and get more."

"Thanks. Oh, and some guy came by to see you earlier. Looked like a bodybuilder. I told him you were out, and I didn't know where. I didn't like his vibes."

My mouth pinched. *Thane.* "It's okay. He found me." Though now I wondered how he'd tracked me down at Herb's.

"Cool. See you when you get back." He hung up.

I turned my pickup around and drove to the Visitor's Bureau, parking beside the small, educational vineyards. A few tourists squelched through the vineyard, thick with long grass. A woman paused to examine the placards identifying the Zinfandel grapes.

I strode to the elegant brick building, vines twining up its high walls. A woman backed from it pulling a stroller. I held the door for her, and she maneuvered through. The baby stretched his hand over the side and dropped his binky to the pavement.

Babies. Something inside me softened. Smiling, I plucked the pacifier from the sidewalk and handed it to her. "I think this is yours."

She laughed. "Thanks."

I walked into the center's high-ceilinged main room. Behind tables displaying t-shirts and corkscrews and decorated glasses, a long tasting bar stretched along the wall.

I didn't see Penny, the lady who ran the bureau, behind the bar. She wasn't in the high-ceilinged room with the viticulture displays either. Nodding to the volunteer behind the bar, I walked down the short hallway to her office.

The door was open. I knocked on its frame and stuck my head inside.

Penny looked up from behind her desk, sheafs of paper in her plump hands. "I can't find my darned glasses."

I pointed. "Your head."

Penny reached up to her fluffy gray hair and pulled the glasses free. Making a face, she slid the glasses on. "That's not the first time I've done that. And it's too much to hope it's the last." She dropped back into her swivel chair, her grape cluster earrings swinging. "So what can I do for you?"

"We're out of maps."

"So soon?" She pointed toward a stack of boxes in the cramped room. "Business must be good."

"It's been picking up." I edged through the maze of wine boxes and opened a smaller box filled with paper maps.

"And I hear you'll soon be expanding." She peered at me over her glasses. "Will we need to change your location on the map?"

My chest hardened. It was a reasonable question. I shouldn't be so touchy about people wondering. I forced a smile. "I'll let you know as soon as I know."

"Don't wait too long. We have to go to the printer next month."

My hands clenched. *Next month?* I was supposed to have a new location by *next month?* I shook my head. I was not going to rush things just to get on the wine map.

"What a terrible thing to happen at that party," she said. "And right after that lovely announcement about the gift to the museum."

I pried a stack of maps from the cardboard box. "Did you know the victim? Chadwick?"

"Only by reputation."

I paused. "What sort of reputation?"

Spots of color darkened her cheeks. "I probably shouldn't say."

I leaned an elbow atop the stack of boxes and raised a brow. "Really?"

"Well..." She plucked at her wine bottle sweater. "The poor man *was* murdered. I suppose it's not *really* gossip."

I bit back a smile. No, we didn't *gossip* in sleepy San Benedetto. Not at all. "Of course not."

She leaned forward, her ample stomach pressing into the desk. "He was having an affair with that volunteer at the Historical Association," she whispered.

My elbow knocked into a cardboard box. I grabbed it before it could fall. "Which one?"

She looked around. I edged backward and closed the office door.

"The married one," she said. "Rea."

"Rea Bobberson?" I asked, my eyes widening. I'd just spoken with her. Maybe she really *did* know something. "How do you know?"

A flush spread down her wrinkled neck. "I accidentally came across them. It was an accident," she said in a rush. "They were in a closet. I'd stopped by and spilled something, and Harriet told me where the cleaning supplies were, and... there they were. There was no mistaking what was going on. Do you think her husband knows?" she asked in a lower tone.

"I hope not," I said. Because if he did, he had good reason to want Chadwick dead. "Have you told the police?"

"It seemed so awkward," she said.

"Still, I think you should."

She sighed. "I suppose so. But do you think Robert will find out? I'd hate to be the one responsible for breaking up a marriage."

"You wouldn't be." That would be on Rea. I hesitated. "Well, thanks for the maps."

"Keep me posted on your new location."

I opened the door. A blond Amazon glared down at me, and I wilted.

"You," Detective Hammer said. "Again."

chapter thirteen

THEY SAY FAMILIARITY BREEDS contempt. But being endlessly harassed by a certain detective had just bred ennui. Laurel and I had been doing this two-step for too many years for me to really be scared. Annoyed, yes. Scared, no.

"Have you heard anything about Belle?" I asked, folding my arms over my hoodie.

Laurel shifted her weight and glanced down the Visitor Center's hallway. "No." She wore a lean, navy pantsuit with bootcut slacks. They hid the boots that would be kicking my backside if I wasn't careful.

"It's true then?" Penny piped up from the desk behind me. "Belle is missing?"

Feminine laughter burst from the tasting room down the hall. And suddenly I wished I was at the bar, swilling wine and joking. It beat hashing out Mason's private life in Penny's cluttered office.

"We don't know," the detective said at the same time I said, "Yes."

Laurel frowned. "It's not that unusual for women to take off when they get cold feet. It's weak and gutless, but not unusual."

She thought Belle was ditching the wedding? "But they don't abandon their kid," I said sharply.

Laurel's blue eyes narrowed. "He's Mason's kid too. Or have you forgotten that?"

My jaw hardened. I hadn't forgotten. Belle and Mason had been young sweethearts. And then he'd joined the military, neither of them knowing she'd been pregnant. She found someone else and hadn't told him about his son.

And then Belle came back into his life, single and with Jordan. And Mason had done the right thing. My throat tightened. So had I by stepping out of the picture, even if it had hurt like hell at the time.

"I suppose it's not *exactly* abandonment." Penny neatened a stack of unfolded wine brochures on her desk. "Not if the child is left with his other parent. Still, it does seem odd. Belle seemed very involved in her son's life."

She had? How did Penny know that? The hair salon wasn't a member of the Visitor's Center. "How well did you know her?" I asked.

"You're not investigating this case, Kosloski." Laurel scowled and pushed past me, and my hip bumped a stack of wine boxes. The bottles inside rattled. "How well did you know Belle Rodale?" the detective demanded.

Penny touched her short gray hair. "She did my hair. We talked about our families."

"Was Belle worried about anything?" I asked. "Was she under any stress?"

"What did I just tell you?" Laurel snarled, moving into my space and forcing me into the hallway. "Beat it."

With one hand, I made a *call-me* gesture to Penny. Laurel slammed the door in my face hard enough to ruffle my hair.

I checked the clock on my phone. It was nearly three, the appointed hour to report in to Mrs. Grandall. And while I, *a)* had better things to do, and *b)* didn't like being ordered around, I *c)* really *did* want to talk to her.

But I, *d)* owed Leo a call. I phoned him from the Visitor's Center parking lot.

"You're not coming back to the museum today," he said without preamble. "Are you?"

Making a guilty face, I leaned against my dusty pickup. I eyed the tourists ambling through the mini vineyard.

"I'm coming back *eventually*," I said. "Just, er, not right now."

"You didn't catch up with Herb either, did you?"

I rubbed the bridge of my nose. Herb could be irritatingly evasive when he wanted. "How'd you guess?"

"Because he stopped by the museum asking about those haunted cow-bells."

"What?" I jerked away from the pickup. Herb had been at the *museum*? *What the hell*? "He wants the binding box they're stored in. You didn't tell them where they were, did you?"

The bells were—according to legend—seriously cursed. They were so cursed, they were kept in a box etched with protective sigils to keep the curse inside and the visitors safe.

I only put the bells out for the holidays. The rest of the year the bells and their box stayed in a cleaning closet in Adele's tearoom, because I'd run out of storage space in the museum. And if Herb had the box...

Actually, I don't know if Herb having the binding box or not helped me. I was just in no mood to make *his* life any easier.

"What do you take me for?" Leo asked indignantly. "Of course I didn't tell him. Why does he want the box?"

"He took the goblet to that shaman, Xavier, to remove the curse that he thinks is on it. Xavier told him the curse was too powerful to remove."

"And those protective boxes aren't easy to find," Leo said. "Huh. Why's the goblet cursed?"

A chill breeze rustled the grapevines in the educational vineyard and tossed my hair. Goose flesh rose on the back of my neck.

Glancing around the lot, I clawed a strand of hair from my eyes. "No idea. But maybe Mrs. Grandall will know."

He snorted. "If you can get an audience."

"She's invited me to meet her at three. Well, she's ordered me to meet her," I corrected.

Leo laughed. "Have fun." He disconnected.

I drove to the oversized, white Victorian where Mrs. Grandall lived and checked the clock on my dash. I was right on time.

Jogging up the porch steps, I rang the bell. It gonged a funereal tone.

After a minute or so, Thane opened the door. His head nearly brushed the top of its frame. Though in fairness, Americans had been a lot shorter when the Victorian had been built.

Thane had paired his black jacket with—I kid you not—tails, black slacks, and a white dress shirt and gloves. The jacket looked a little tight in the shoulders.

"You're the butler too?" I asked brightly.

He glowered. "Tanis is out sick."

"Bummer. So," I said. "Mrs. Grandall wanted to see me?"

"She can't. She's busy."

"You said three o'clock," I said, annoyed. "It's three o'clock."

"Her plans changed."

My face tightened. "She could have called." So maybe I *was* only a paranormal museum owner. My time was important too. And, okay, maybe this visit hadn't taken me *that* far out of my way. But it had still wasted my time.

"Her plans changed," he repeated.

"Is she home?"

"Her—"

"Plans changed," I finished for him. What about *my* plans?

"Thane!" she yelled from somewhere inside the house. His blond head whipped toward the sound.

I darted past the oversized gorilla, my tennis shoes soft on the parquet floor. If Mrs. Grandall was going to bug out on the meeting *she'd* called, she was going to tell me to my face.

"Hey," he shouted at me.

"Thane," she called again.

I oriented on the sound and speedwalked down a hall lined with portraits of sullen ancestors. Skidding to a halt in front of a set of high, double doors, I grasped their brass handles.

"Thane!"

Wrenching open the doors, the trainer hot on my heels, I stopped short. Thane barreled into me. I staggered into a fancy exercise bike.

Mrs. Grandall, in a pink t-shirt and tights, lay on a long, wooden bench-type thing. Her legs were in the air and caught in two straps. She glared. "I'm stuck."

Thane hurried forward. Gently, he released one foot from the contraption, then the other. He helped the white-haired woman to sitting.

"Pilates," she said to me, then frowned at Thane. "And I asked not to be disturbed."

"We had an appointment," I said.

"Did we?" Mrs. Grandall cocked her head. "Oh, my. I forgot. I'm so sorry," she said insincerely.

"He didn't forget." I nodded to Thane.

"Was he being overprotective? You must forgive him. He's like a son to me." She beamed at the big goon. "So much so, that I'm adopting him. Now, have you found that goblet?"

Adoption? Ew. Thane had to be in his mid-thirties, at least. "Not yet. Herb said it's cursed."

Thane handed her a white hand towel.

She patted the back of her neck with it. "Herb Linden? That lunatic who stole my goblet? I'm not surprised he's come up with some ridiculous story. The man's obsessed."

It takes one obsessed collector to know one. "You know more about the goblet's history than me. *Could* it be cursed?"

"Of course not." Mrs. Grandall snorted and blotted her forehead. "What an idea."

"But there must have been some reason why Clayton Clarke's father kept it in his paranormal collection," I reasoned.

"Solomon Clarke was a thief, as you should know. Everyone knows he stole an artifact from Ladies Aid. Did they ever get that statuette back?"

My shoulder muscles tightened. "Yes." It had been evidence in a murder investigation, but the police had eventually returned it. "I'm sure Solomon kept records of his acquisitions though. Maybe there'll be more details about this curse in his files."

"So-*called* curse," she snapped. "There's nothing wrong with that—" She exhaled heavily and smiled. "Thank you for your report, Maddie. You may go."

I turned to the door, then turned back. "Before I do, have you found a laptop bag?"

"A laptop bag?" Her white brows lowered.

"Left somewhere at your house," I said. "After the party."

"Did you lose a laptop bag?" She dropped her towel beside her on the Pilates machine. "I'll ask the maid to look for it."

"No," I said. "Chadwick was seen here at the party with the bag. I just wondered what had happened to it."

"Isn't that a question the police should be asking?" she said pointedly.

"I'm sure they will." My smile was brief. "I'll let you know what I find out about the goblet."

It wasn't until I reached the Victorian's porch steps that I realized she hadn't confirmed or denied finding a laptop bag. I hesitated. But the implication had been clear. She hadn't seen the bag.

The phone rang in the pocket of my paranormal museum hoodie. I checked the number. *Leo.* "Hey, I'm on—"

"There's a flood in the main room," he said in a panicked tone. "Water's coming from the ceiling."

I froze. *From the ceiling?* Mason and Belle lived above the museum. The water had to either be coming from their apartment, or the museum had some very weird plumbing.

"I'll be right there." I disconnected, raced to my pickup, and called Mason. *Answer, answer, answer.*

It went to voicemail. *Augh!*

"There's water coming from the ceiling of the museum," I said. "There may be a problem in your apartment."

I climbed into my pickup and drove as fast as I could down the country roads to the town. There was an empty parking spot in front of the museum, and though those spots were reserved for civilians, I screeched into it. I raced into the museum, the bell jangling above the door.

GD hissed from the top of the old-fashioned register. Chest heaving, I stopped to assess the situation.

A waterfall spewed from the ceiling. It splashed over the black crown molding and flowed down the white wall.

Water puddled on the floor and glinted in Leo's dark hair. He'd dragged several shelves away from the wall. Scuffs on the checkerboard tiles marked their path.

He gulped. "Help."

"I'll be right back." I ran to Mason's motorcycle shop next door and blasted through the glass door.

Mason paced behind the counter, cell phone pressed to his ear. Custom-built bikes gleamed on the gray carpet.

"Mason," I hissed.

He shook his head.

"There's a flood in your apartment," I said more loudly.

"What?" He lowered the phone.

"Water's coming through the museum's ceiling."

Mason swore. "I'll call you back." He jammed the phone into the rear pocket of his black jeans and raced into the back room. There was a door to the alley through there, I knew, and a staircase leading up to his apartment.

I didn't follow. If the water was coming from Mason's apartment, he'd deal with it. And if it wasn't, he'd let me know I had a bigger problem.

Shaking my head, I hurried to the tearoom. Adele looked up from the reservation book and smiled at me from behind the hostess stand. "You're just in time for afternoon tea."

"There's a flood in the museum," I rapped out. "I need towels."

Her coffee eyes widened. Wordlessly, she pivoted and raced into the hallway. I followed more slowly and nearly collided with her emerging from the kitchen. She thrust a stack of towels into my arms. "I'll get a mop," she said.

I strode to the bookcase and pressed the special spine. The secret door pivoted inward, and I trotted into the museum.

Leo had moved the haunted rocking chair and a few more shelves out of the way of the flow of water. I handed him half the towels.

"The haunted photos." He nodded toward the black and white photos of murderers and their victims lining the wall.

Water blurred their images. Something hard and cold and painful hooked my chest.

The photos were ruined.

chapter fourteen

DULLY, I STARED AT the blurred photo and wiped its black frame with a paper towel. An ache squeezed my chest. *Cora McBride*. The black and white image had bubbled, brownish streaks marring Cora's face.

The loss of a few photos shouldn't matter. Thanks to Clayton's donation, I now had plenty of other exhibits to show. But I blinked back tears, as I set the framed photo along with the stack of others on the haunted rocking chair.

I told myself it was only an old photo. But it had been the first paranormal mystery I'd solved at the museum, the first artifact I'd really dug into researching.

The water had stopped running down the wall, by which I presumed Mason had turned off the flow upstairs. I'd mopped the puddle of dirty water on the floor, but the checkerboard tiles were still slick.

Someone knocked at the museum door. I frowned. I'd closed the museum. The floor was a hazard, and I didn't have the bandwidth to deal with customers *and* a flood.

I set my mop against the damp wall. Mason stood framed behind the upper pane of glass. I walked to the door and unlocked it.

"How bad is it?" Mason asked.

Leo, wiping the wall with a towel, turned and glared. "Bad enough."

On the glass front counter, GD meowed. The black cat flicked his tail.

"There's no damage to the floor, I think." That was the benefit of cheap linoleum. "But the wall will need to dry out. The leak came from your apartment?"

Mason nodded and blew out his breath. "Would you come upstairs with me?"

Why? He knew I didn't have any plumbing chops. But I said, "Sure," and followed him to the bookcase door. We walked through it into the tearoom and down the bamboo hallway.

Adele popped out of her kitchen. "How is it?" She wiped her hands on her pristine white apron.

"I think we're okay," I said.

"I called Dieter," she said. "He's bringing over fans and heat lamps and some sort of treatment to make sure nothing molds."

I smiled, pressing my fingers to my lips. Being married to a contractor had its advantages. Dieter had been a handyman before marrying Adele. Since the wedding, he'd stepped up his game.

"Thanks," I said. "You're a lifesaver." Though since Adele owned the building, technically she was helping herself out too.

"He'll come up to your apartment too," she told Mason.

He grunted. "Thanks."

"What happened?" she burst out.

"Sink overflowed," he said.

Adele angled her head. "What—?"

"I'll explain later," he said. Taking my arm, he steered me down the hallway to the heavy, metal door at the end. We exited into the brick alley.

Curious, I followed him up narrow, concrete stairs to the studded security door. He opened it, and we walked inside.

Watery sunlight streamed through the massive skylight over the studio's industrial-chic living area. The furniture was white, black, and modern, the walls bare brick, the floors distressed.

Square, glass bricks divided the bedroom from the living area. Jordan's clothes lay scattered across the sofa. I hadn't considered how cramped the studio must be for the three of them.

The kitchen was open plan. Cereal boxes and unwashed bowls and smaller, colorful boxes dotted its stainless steel counter. A mop leaned against it.

"It happened here." He nodded toward the kitchen.

I walked to the counter. The smaller boxes were from a hair dye kit. I glanced at him, his long, blond hair done up in its usual neat ponytail.

"The sink was running," he said. "It wasn't plugged, but it drains slow. It probably took thirty minutes or so for it to fill up and overflow."

My heart dropped. "Belle was here." She'd been here and had made sure to avoid Mason.

"And she left in a hurry."

It had been some hurry if she hadn't had time to turn off the water tap. I picked up the box and read the label. *Black Ice*. Dread coiled in my gut. Belle had come here, dyed her hair, and ran. "Did she take anything?"

"I think so. Check the sleeping area."

I walked around the glass bricks. Two drawers in the bureau were open—lingerie and tops. Belle's clothing inside was disarranged. "I think you should call the police."

He came to stand beside me. "If I do, they'll stop looking for her."

Because she hadn't been taken. Belle was on the run. But from what? What she'd seen that night at the mansion? But then why hadn't she gone to the police? They'd keep her safe.

"They'll want to talk to her about the murder." I gave a slight head shake. "I don't think they'll stop looking, even if she left voluntarily."

"Wait to tell him."

Surprised, I looked up at Mason. *Tell who? Jason?*

"I know you have to tell him. You're too honest not to say anything. But wait until you see him next. Don't call him about this."

I swallowed, and I nodded. I could put off telling Jason. For a little while.

Dieter set up heat lamps and fans aimed at the sodden wall and made me promise to leave them running all night. It would do wonders for my electric bill. But I couldn't infect my visitors with black mold, so reluctantly, I agreed.

I sent Leo home. GD curled up beside a heat lamp.

At loose ends, I drove to Ladies Aid. If anyone knew the gossip on a local curse, it would be someone there. Not that the ladies were interested in curses, per se. But they were definitely interested in gossip. It was the lodge's power source, its life energy, its *mana*.

I parked in the lot of the two-story, fifties era building and walked to the black door. I swung the knocker hung below the Ladies Aid crest, inset with brass California poppies.

After a few minutes, Cora, in a purple kaftan, opened the door. "Why Maddie, this is a surprise. What brings you to Ladies Aid?"

"Oral history."

Her round face crinkled in a smile. "Gossip, you mean? Come inside." She held the door wider.

I walked into a hall lined with photos of Ladies Aid presidents past and present. Each wore a blue robe and held a white rose. There was no doubt some deep symbolism around both, and I didn't want to know what it was.

Against one wall, a glass-fronted cabinet glittered with awards. I studied the design in the linoleum floor: a set of tiles with the astrological glyph for Venus, a bee, and a rose.

"The bee represents Venus," Cora said. "The goddess, not the planet. Come into the sitting room."

She led me down the hall to a set of double doors and pushed them wide. I followed her inside a room covered in rose-patterned wallpaper.

Bookshelves and paintings lined the walls. A few older women sat knitting in groupings of high-backed chairs.

"What sort of gossip are you looking for?" Cora asked.

"Historical. Anything to do with the Benedetto goblet."

Her mouth pursed. "You haven't found it yet, I take it?"

"No, but I'll get it back." I furrowed my brow. "Herb seems to think it's cursed. I'm trying to figure out why."

"Hm." She scanned the room. Her gaze settled on a comfortably padded, white-haired woman in a fuzzy white sweater and pink sweatpants. Her gnarled hands were busy knitting something orange and gold. "I think... Anne might be a good person to ask."

Cora strode toward the woman. "Anne, have you got a moment?"

Anne looked up and grinned. "Time's all I've got these days. What can I do you for?"

"This is—"

"Madelyn Kosloski," Anne said. "I was at your baptism, though I don't suppose you remember."

My face warmed. "No."

Anne laughed. "And I don't suppose you remember kicking Pastor Roth right in the chin either?"

I didn't, but I'd heard the story often enough. It had long since ceased being funny, but I smiled anyway.

"Don't feel bad," she said. "He deserved it. But we don't always get what we deserve, do we? Speaking of which, what are you intending to do with your new museum?"

I scraped my hands through my hair. "New—? Oh, the donation. I haven't really gotten around to thinking about a whole new museum yet."

"Then you'd better start." Anne set her knitting in the cloth bag beside her chair.

"Maddie has questions about the Benedetto goblet," Cora said. "I'll let you two talk." She moved toward a table where a samovar stood.

"I heard about that mess too." The old lady's eyes twinkled. "Has Herb given it up yet?"

"No," I said sourly. "He seems to think it's cursed."

"What nonsense. There's no such thing as curses. No offense to your museum." She inclined her head.

I sat in the wingchair across from her. "What history might have given him the idea that there is a curse attached?"

Anne canted her head and pursed her lips. "I don't recall any ghost stories about that goblet, if that's what you mean."

"I'm not sure what I mean," I confessed. But in my experience, curses and ghost stories were often contradictory and flexible. They stretched to fit the situation or the teller. Keeping my questions vague was actually part of my process.

"That's the problem with history," she said. "The news reports of the day were no more reliable than our own. And when we don't have documentary evidence, we guess. Take Benedetto himself—the man who immigrated to California, not the saint. What do we really know about him?"

"We know he had one of the first vineyards in the area."

Anne cocked her head. "Did he now?"

Shifting, I crossed my legs and braced one elbow on an arm of the wingchair. Anne was hinting at something, but she seemed to expect me to work for the answer. "That's what I learned in school."

"But who did he get his vineyard from?"

"The land, you mean?" I frowned. "I assumed... Who owned it when he came here from Italy? There were native tribes in California. But their rights were pretty well ignored by the settlers. It wasn't nice or pretty, but it's what was going on at the time."

Teacups rattled. We glanced toward Cora and the samovar.

"And then came the Spanish," Anne continued, "with their land grants. And then Mexico for about twenty years, and then the Americans took charge." She bent and retrieved her knitting.

"Yes," I said, bewildered by the rehash of California history. "Did Vincenzo buy the land—or steal it—from someone with a Spanish land grant?"

"Not steal, no. He bought it fair and square from a widow. Well, fair and square except for the price." Her mouth made a moue of regret. "She got enough to return to Spain with her children, and I'll wager she was happy to just get gone. But Vincenzo Benedetto got a deal on that land. And for the record, there was already a vineyard on it when he took over."

So his hadn't been the first vineyard. "How do you know all this?"

"I used to be a history teacher, dear. That was when history—delving into facts and evidence—*meant* something. I delved," Anne said with a satisfied air. "But of course no one wanted to hear that Benedetto's wasn't the first vineyard. It ruined the story of the town with his name."

"It was a long time ago. I suppose in the end, it doesn't really matter."

Anne jerked forward and smacked her hand on the arm of the chair. "Of course it matters. Facts matter. The truth matters. So what if it's a minor historical detail? It's history, true history. And if we don't know our history, we're doomed to repeat the bad parts."

"And those who *do* know history are doomed to watch it being repeated." And it did repeat. Personal history. National history. World history. We never learned. We just went round and round.

She laughed and settled back in her chair. "You have no idea just how depressing that is. But it's preferable to ignorance."

"So you really don't know why the goblet may have a curse story attached to it?"

Anne scratched her rounded chin with the tip of a knitting needle. "I don't think he was a very *nice* man, our Benedetto. I did a good bit of research into local history, as you may have surmised. It's not what was said about him in the historical records. It's what *wasn't* said. Do you understand?"

"I think so," I said slowly. "But you don't know anything concrete?"

"Nothing curse-worthy, I'm afraid. Will knowing the story help you find the goblet?"

"No," I admitted. "It's just... a knowledge gap. And I don't like those."

She smiled. "Perhaps there's more to you and your paranormal museum than I thought. Invite me to your grand opening. I may not believe in the paranormal, but I do like a good story."

chapter fifteen

"WHAT DO YOU MEAN it didn't work?" Aghast, I stared down at Dieter, crouching on the floor beside the stained wall. GD lay coiled beside a space heater, its filaments glowing, his eyes closed.

The contractor ran a hand over his spiky brown hair. Dieter stood and hitched up his paint-stained coveralls. "I'm saying I'm going to need to replace this drywall. The good news is I can do it today. I'll have you back up and running this afternoon, if you don't mind the paint smell."

I rubbed my forehead. What choice did I have? "Fine. And thanks."

I hated for the museum to be closed. Thursday mornings we started to get busy. Not as busy as the weekends, but still. The museum was a time-killer for tourists before the wineries opened.

I called Leo and told him not to come in until the afternoon. Then I left Dieter to his work. I hesitated outside Mason's motorcycle shop. It had a CLOSED sign in the window as well. Grimacing, I continued to my red pickup.

If Rea and Chadwick had been having an affair, there would be gossip. There was *always* gossip. I'd already tapped the local Historical Association, but there was one other source available. I drove to Sacramento.

The freeway was thick with fog, slowing my progress, big rigs looming suddenly out of the gray mass. I caught myself leaning forward, my hands tensing on the wheel. When I finally exited, I exhaled slowly, the muscles between my shoulder blades releasing.

I made my way to the ACHA's neighborhood. Mist hung low above the trees and the prairie-style homes. I parked on the street. Crossing the lawn, I climbed the concrete steps and knocked on the ACHA's green door.

When no one answered, I tried the knob and walked inside. My footsteps were noiseless on the pale, floral-patterned rug.

"Hello?" I called.

A slender woman in slacks and a blue sweater appeared at the top of the stairs carrying a stack of papers. She looked to be about my age, her auburn hair tied in a neat ponytail bound by a scarf. "Can I help you?" With her free hand, she adjusted her tortoiseshell glasses.

The stack of documents exploded from her arm. Papers fluttered down the dark-wood stairwell. "Oh!" she cried.

I hurried to help pick up the fallen pages.

"This is a disaster," she said, crouching beside a potted fern to gather more papers. "I had them all collated for the presentation."

I glanced at a page. It looked like a plan to attract donations. Which was totally normal and the sort of thing I'd need to think about if I turned the museum into a non-profit. *Ugh.*

"When's the presentation?" I asked with forced cheerfulness.

She groaned. "In thirty minutes."

"I'll help you sort them." I began laying the papers I'd gathered into stacks on the thin carpet.

"It's not your job." She glanced up the stairs. "You don't have to."

"I don't have anything better to do this morning. There was a flood in my museum, and it's temporarily shut down."

She gathered more pages. "Which museum?"

"The paranormal museum in San Benedetto." I fished out a business card and handed it to her.

Taking it, she sat back on her heels. "But I've been to that museum. It's a lot of fun. A little behind the times, but—" She flushed. "Sorry."

"You don't have to apologize. You're not wrong." I spotted a paper beneath the vacant reception desk and slithered forward to retrieve it. "Have you heard about our big donation?"

"Dr. MacDuff did mention something about it."

I paused. Had I imagined her emphasis on the man's title? "We've been offered a sizable collection of paranormal antiques and vintage objects.

There's one in particular I'm trying to learn more about, the Benedetto goblet."

The goblet wasn't why I was here, but it made a decent excuse. Though I would eventually need to learn more about it. I hoped there'd be more info on why Clayton's father had thought it was paranormal back at the warehouse.

"We don't do research here," she said. "We merely support other historical associations."

"But Chadwick was doing research on the goblet. I was hoping to take a look at what he'd learned."

"Dr. MacDuff won't even let me inside the closet Chadwick was using as an office. I'm afraid you're out of luck."

I had *not* imagined the emphasis. While I arranged papers, I studied her covertly. Twin spots of color darkened her cheeks.

"I understand Chadwick's laptop is missing?" I said.

She froze, one hand poised above a stack of papers.

I gathered up two stacks and rose. "The police are looking for it." I walked to the wooden desk and set the papers atop it, then I turned to her.

She remained crouched on the carpet, her expression hard. "They won't find it. Not before *Dr.* MacDuff gets at it, if he hasn't already."

I frowned. "What do you mean?"

She adjusted her glasses and glanced at the stairs to the second floor. "I mean Chadwick wrote MacDuff's PhD dissertation," she said in a low voice. "It's maddening. What's the good of a PhD if you didn't write your own dissertation?"

I leaned one hip against the desk. "Why would Chadwick do that?" I asked, matching her quiet tone. "Wasn't Chadwick busy enough working on his own dissertation?"

She gathered up more stacks of papers and stood. "He was paid, of course."

"By MacDuff? I didn't think Chadwick needed the money." Not with a winery inheritance. Unless the old joke about wineries was true. *How do you make a million dollars on a vineyard? Start with two million dollars.*

"And I'm sure MacDuff promised an excellent reference." Her voice was thick with disgust.

"But it's cheating," I said, straightening off the desk. "Why would Chadwick help with something like that?"

"MacDuff is a fine director. But the board wanted the director of the ACHA to have a PhD, which MacDuff didn't have. Chadwick probably thought the requirement was ridiculous. And I suppose it is. You don't need a credential to do the job. MacDuff's been managing fine without one. But it's important to the donors."

"How did you find out?" Because if Chadwick had helped him cheat, and MacDuff wanted it kept secret... It might just be a motive for murder.

She angled her head and gave me a wry look. "Admin assistants know *everything.*"

She wasn't wrong about that. I'd learned early in my career not to take the admins for granted. "I wonder if Rea would know anything about Chadwick's research?" I asked casually and wandered toward the stairs. If only I could get into his office, see his work...

"Rea? Rea Bobberson?" She frowned. "I doubt it."

I turned to the woman. "I understood they worked closely together at the San Benedetto Historical Association."

She laid out the stacks of papers on the reception desk and began collating them. "I hadn't heard that."

I lounged against the paneled wall. *So much for knowing everything.* Unless she was covering for the dead man. "Do you know where I could find Rea?"

"She lives near your museum. Rea and Robert restored a lovely old Victorian." She pulled a phone from her hip pocket. "I'll text you their contacts."

"Why do you want to talk to Rea Bobberson?" a man boomed from the stairs, and we started.

The woman's hand spasmed. She crumpled the pages she held.

Dr. MacDuff descended the rest of the stairs. "Aren't those ready yet?" His salt and pepper hair was slicked back today. His green tie was knotted tightly about his collar. The tie didn't quite match his suit jacket.

"They'll be ready," she said.

"They won't be if you waste more time gossiping," he warned, stepping closer. He smelled of coconut, a scent I normally enjoy, but on him it just seemed rancid.

"She wasn't gossiping," I said coolly. "I was. But surely the rumors about Rea and Bob Bobberson are false," I said, fishing.

"Of course they're false," he huffed. "Robert and his wife are devoted to each other."

Ah, ha. There *was* something going on in their marriage—or outside it.

"Besides," he continued, "the way their finances are entwined, a divorce would be catastrophic. Julie, you know better," he scolded.

Entwined finances? Who was gossiping now?

The woman's lips compressed. "I'll just finish collating these upstairs." She snatched up the stacks of papers and hurried up the steps.

"Who would the divorce be more catastrophic for, do you think?" I asked. "Robert or Rea?"

His hazel eyes narrowed. "I don't gossip, and especially not about our board members. What are you doing here?"

"Has Chadwick's laptop turned up? I'm desperate to see his research on the Benedetto goblet."

His oval face reddened. "No. And when it does, any work on it is the property of the ACHA."

"Right. Has anyone else been asking about it?"

"Aside from the police? No. Why do you ask?"

"No reason. Thanks." I hurried out the door and to my pickup, parked on the street.

Inside, I drummed my fingers on the wheel. So a divorce would have been disastrous? Yet Rea had risked one by dallying with Chadwick.

My cell phone vibrated, and I checked the screen. A text from an unknown number with a shared contact attached. I glanced at the house-turned-office and smiled. *Thanks, Julie.*

I craned my neck upward and peered at the unremitting mercury sky. Half a dozen crows sat like musical notes on the electric wires. If I'd had any foresight, I would have chosen a different metaphor—that their ebony contours were an *I Ching* predicting doom.

chapter sixteen

I'D LIKE TO SAY I was going with the flow, letting the universe unfold, and being Zen about the museum closure. But I was really just mad.

The museum shouldn't have been closed on a Thursday. And if this was the universe nudging me into finding a new location, I resented the nudge.

But fuming wasn't going to do me any good, so I went to find Herb. Staking out his mother's house was a no-go. Not if she was keeping that shotgun beside the front door.

Also, Herb probably wasn't home at this hour. He had a number of places where he stashed the objects he collected. I only knew of one, but it seemed as good a place as any to watch.

After stopping in the museum to check on GD, I left town. I drove across the railroad tracks, past several vineyards, and into an industrial park. Fading tan paint peeled off the corrugated metal buildings. Weeds grew through the pavement cracks.

A yellow VW bug sat parked in front of a wooden door, and I exhaled with satisfaction. *Herb.*

Smiling, I strode to the keypad beside the door. I punched in a number I'd seen him enter in once and which I had filed away for future reference. To my delighted surprise, a latch clicked, and the light on the keypad blinked green.

I edged the door open and walked inside a room stacked with neatly labeled boxes. Tagged paranormal objects sat upon rows of shelves built into the walls. Security cameras gazed down, blinking red, from the corners of the room. I waved at one and walked deeper into the warehouse.

Long and narrow, it wasn't as big as the warehouse belonging to Clayton's father. But Herb had managed to create two aisles stacked high with boxes.

Cardboard slithered across concrete. I followed the sound.

Herb pried open an oversized cardboard box—the type movers use—and leaned inside.

"Hi, Herb."

He yelped and jerked away. The little man pressed one hand to his bow tie. "How'd you get in here?"

"Witchcraft. Where's the goblet?"

He stiffened. Light from an overhead lamp glinted off his thick glasses. "You'll never find it. Also, it's not here. Have you reconsidered about Dion Fortune's scrying mirror? My buyer had some financial difficulties, and it's still available."

"Since when did you start trafficking in stolen goods?"

"I'm not trafficking the goblet." His nose twitched. "That would be unethical."

I jammed my hands on my hips. "Versus stealing it?"

"You left me no choice in the matter."

I scowled. What had I had to do with it? And he'd had plenty of choices. He still did. "Don't try to blame me. Now why do you think it's cursed?"

His expression turned shifty. "Who told you that?"

"Xavier."

"Oh. Well." He braced a hand on the edge of the open box. "It's complicated."

"Then uncomplicate it," I snarled. "Mrs. Grandall and all of Ladies Aid are on my case about getting it back."

He shuddered. "The history is a little vague. So vague, some would say it's only a rumor."

"Like pretty much everything else in my museum. What's the story?"

He shook his head. "No. It's too dangerous."

"The story's too dangerous?" I asked sharply. I didn't have time for this drama. "That's not because it's..." *Wait.* Chadwick had been researching the goblet. Chadwick was dead. Maybe Herb *wasn't* being a drama queen. "It's not connected to the recent murder, is it?"

His eyes widened behind his thick glasses. "Of course not. I mean. Well, maybe. I suppose it could have influenced—but no. It was safely in that warehouse. It couldn't have had anything to do with Chadwick's death."

"Let's talk about Chadwick." I braced an elbow on a stack of boxes. "Did you know him?"

Herb nodded. "A bit. He came to me asking about any urban legends around Vincenzo Benedetto."

"And you told him about the goblet," I guessed. That explained Chadwick's research. "Is it valuable?"

"What?"

"The goblet."

"No, I told you, it's cursed."

For Pete's sake. Cursed smursed. "Cursed *how?*"

He folded his arms over his tweed jacket. "I won't say. You think you understand curses, but you've only scratched the surface. Sometimes, with certain curses, when you think about them, when you talk about them, you make them stronger. You give them power."

"You told Chadwick about the curse," I said, accusing.

"No, I didn't."

I frowned, puzzled. "Why not? And don't tell me the story's too dangerous. Because we both know that's bunk."

"Because I didn't know the whole story. I still don't. And I think Chadwick knew more than I did," he muttered.

"Then why do you think the goblet is so cursed it needs a curse box to hold it?"

"Because I can *feel* that. Any good paranormal collector could."

My gaze flicked toward the flat metal ceiling. Herb had nothing. I stepped closer and held out one hand. "Whatever. Hand it over."

The little man quailed. "You can't make me," he squeaked. "It isn't right."

"Stealing the goblet wasn't right," I said loudly, but my chest twinged with guilt. And why should I feel guilty? Herb was the one who'd stolen the goblet. "Give me that goblet, or I'm getting the cops involved."

Herb paled. "You wouldn't," he croaked, hands trembling. "You can't. The goblet's dangerous. No one can handle it until it's safely boxed."

I glared at my collector. He cringed against the high box. And suddenly I felt like a rat. Worse than a rat. I felt like...

Like Detective Laurel Hammer, sure of the rightness of my cause and the wrongness of Herb's. My shoulders collapsed. Hot tingling swept from my neck to my face. "Herb—"

He pivoted and bolted down the aisle.

"Herb!"

A metal door clanged. I ground my teeth. There must be a door at the rear of the warehouse too. But his escape wasn't what bothered me. What bothered me was me.

I trudged to the front of the metal warehouse. Making sure the door was locked behind me, I walked to my pickup and climbed inside.

I drummed my fingers on the wheel. I didn't *like* feeling like Laurel. It made me more sympathetic toward the detective, which I didn't enjoy. I preferred to think of her as a one-dimensional villain, even though I knew it was ridiculous.

And I *really* didn't want to act like her. But I had. A burst of raindrops pattered on the pickup's roof and splashed the windshield.

I also didn't want to think about this all day, and I knew I would if I didn't distract myself. So I called Mason.

He answered on the first ring. "Find anything?" he asked.

"No," I said guiltily. "I was just calling to see if you had."

"No." He paused. "Have you told Jason she was here yet?"

"I haven't seen him," I hedged. Threatening Herb. Withholding information in a criminal investigation from Jason... What had happened to me?

"Thanks. There is one thing. Belle made a phone call from our apartment's land line." He recited a number. "I've tried calling, but no one answers. I just get a message that the voicemail for this number is full."

"Hold on." Setting the phone on the dash, I put it on speaker and scrolled to my notes section. "Can you repeat that number?"

He did, and I sucked in a slow breath. "That belongs to the Bobbersons. Or at least to one of them if you're getting a full voicemail message."

"The Bobbersons. You mean... the guy we met at the ACHA?" He swore. "There is a connection between those people and Belle."

And to the murder. I started my truck. "You need to call Laurel Hammer. Now. This is important."

"Right. I'll make the call." He hung up.

Thanks to the nice lady at the ACHA, I not only knew Rea and Bob Bobberson lived in San Benedetto, I had their address. I plugged their contact info into my phone's map app and aimed my pickup toward their house.

I knew I shouldn't go. Mason was calling the cops. They'd no doubt want to have a word with the Bobbersons themselves. But I had an idea about the goblet, and I wanted Rea to confirm it before she got tied up in a police interrogation.

My pickup bumped over the railroad tracks. I swayed in my seat.

Herb had said he didn't know the whole story, that Chadwick had known more. But I suspected Herb hadn't believed the goblet was haunted until *after* he'd spoken with Chadwick. That might explain Herb's vagueness about the supposed curse.

I turned down a wide road between vineyards. A shaft of sunlight slipped from between the clouds and vanished.

If Chadwick had given Herb anything concrete, I was fairly certain Herb would have told me. He loved showing off his paranormal knowledge. But maybe Chadwick had confided in his lover. Who might be about to get hauled off to the SBPD.

So I wasn't interfering in an investigation. I was conducting my own, personal investigation into the goblet. Showing up on Rea's doorstep in that light was totally normal and understandable. I had to get to her before the cops did, or who knew when I'd get a chance?

The Bobbersons lived at the end of a wide expanse of lawn in a massive brick house. Fog blurred its gabled roofline. I parked in the driveway beside a silver Mercedes. Since I'd seen her husband driving a sports car, I hoped this was Rea's.

I climbed brick steps to a white front door. A knocker in the shape of a lion snarled at me. Ignoring it, I rang the bell.

It gonged deep inside the house. I waited a couple minutes, shifting my weight, then rang the bell again. I waited a few more minutes, then called the number the ACHA receptionist had given me.

The phone rang. There was a faint echo from inside the house. It rang five times, then I got the full voicemail message.

I pursed my lips. Rea couldn't be too far away if I could hear her phone.

I lifted the ring on the door knocker and banged it. The door shifted inward. Warm, vanilla-scented air billowed from the house.

Crap. Briefly, I closed my eyes. An unanswered phone. An open door. A murder suspect. My shoulders curled inward, my heartbeat turning sluggish.

Using my fingertips, I pushed the door wider. Maybe Rea'd had a heart attack. Maybe she'd fallen down the stairs and couldn't get up. I dried my sweaty palms down the front of my jeans. "Mrs. Bobberson?" I called. "Rea?"

A narrow table on my right held keys, a rolled pair of sports socks, and a pink pot of lip balm. An owl-shaped air-freshener glowed from an outlet beneath the table.

I stepped inside a carpeted hall and stopped short. Rea lay sprawled on the floral carpet at the base of the stairs. I took a step toward her and recoiled. A thick green cord was knotted around her neck.

chapter seventeen

"WHY ARE YOU HERE?" Laurel's arctic eyes crackled with fury. She leaned closer.

I took a step backward and my foot landed on an outsized stone on the home's gravel path. It twisted beneath my heel, and I stumbled, chilled by the fog and Laurel's question.

Why was I here? The question had started to take on existential dimensions. Why? What was my purpose in life? What was my purpose at all? And even though she hadn't meant the question in a metaphysical way, hearing it from her just made me mad.

"If I'd known Rea was dead," I said, "I wouldn't have come."

It was a terrible answer. I glanced guiltily at Jason.

Arms folded, he stood expressionless beside a box hedge in his navy suit. Jason hadn't said much to me since his arrival. Behind him, uniformed officers moved in and out of the brick house.

"Why?" Laurel snarled.

Because I'm stubborn to the point of stupidity. I scrubbed a hand over my face. "I wanted to ask Rea about the Benedetto goblet."

Her nostrils flared. "The what?"

"A strange goblet that once belonged to Vincenzo Benedetto," I said. "It somehow wound up in the paranormal collection Clayton's donating to the museum. Herb ran off with it—he seems to think it's a little too cursed. He told me Chadwick had been researching the goblet. But since Chadwick's dead and the ACHA can't seem to find his research, I thought Rea might know something."

"Why?" Jason asked. "Why would she know anything about it?"

"Because they, er, worked together at the Historical Association. Closely. And Penny said she saw them kissing," I blurted.

Jason rubbed his temple. "Penny? Penny Beauvais from the Visitor's Center?"

"She didn't mention it to you?" I asked weakly. "Yesterday I told her she should. You *saw* her. We were in her office together." Until Laurel had kicked me out.

Laurel's jaw clenched. "Well she didn't. After I left, she called while I was in the driving back to the station," she said through gritted teeth. "She left a message that she wanted to talk. But she didn't say why."

"We'll speak to Penny later," Jason said. "Is there anyone *else* who should be talking to us?" He asked pointedly.

Laurel looked past me and cursed. "The husband's here."

I glanced over my shoulder. A silver Lexus parked in the driveway. The driver's door opened. Bob Bobberson bolted from the car, the ends of his suit jacket flapping around his broad hips. "Rea," he shouted. "Where is she?"

Laurel strode across the lawn and intercepted him. She said something to Bob. He swayed then folded over, his hands on his knees.

"Did you know about Belle?" Jason asked, his tone lowering. "That she'd been back to their apartment?"

"Yes. I asked Mason to report it." But that wasn't the whole story, and it wasn't completely honest. His real question was when had I known? And I knew exactly why I was dodging the answer.

"There was a flood in the museum yesterday," I continued. "The water was coming from upstairs, and I told Mason. He turned off the water in his apartment. Then he showed me what he'd found."

"Why didn't you tell me?" he asked, voice hard.

"I thought Mason should." I tugged at the collar of my hoodie. "He said he would."

"He did. An hour ago. She was in their apartment yesterday, and I only found out about it today."

"I'm sorry," I said and wondered why I was really apologizing. "Do you have any idea where Belle is?"

He glanced toward the gabled house. "No."

My heart sank lower. The police thought Belle was involved with Rea's murder. And if she was involved with Rea's, then odds were...

"Belle couldn't have killed Chadwick," I muttered. "It doesn't make sense. There's no connection aside from them both being at the party."

A coroner's black van pulled to the curb.

"She cut Chadwick's hair," Jason said.

I started. "What?" Mason hadn't mentioned that. But maybe he didn't know. Why *would* he know about all Belle's clients?

"Mason didn't tell you?" He laughed mirthlessly. "He told me."

My mouth compressed. So. Mason had been withholding information from me too. And I'd been withholding information from Jason. Jason had been the only honest actor in the whole affair. At least he told me when there were things he couldn't tell me. Though I wish he'd have mentioned Belle's disappearance sooner.

"I should have called you yesterday. I'm sorry," I repeated.

He sighed. "That's one of the problems with amateur detecting. You don't have policies you have to follow. The rules keep us honest. They keep the information flowing, even when we'd rather protect the people we care about."

"That wasn't—" I bit off my denial. I'd left it to Mason to tell the cops, so I'd have a chance to ask Rea about the goblet. "Belle isn't a killer."

But the fact that she was in the wind, that she'd run, that she'd dyed her hair to change her appearance, did not look good. I rubbed my eyebrow. "I told Rea to talk to you too."

"You met her?" he asked. "When was this? What did she tell you?"

"She came by the museum yesterday. She thought I had an in with the cops—with you, I guess—and she had confidential information about Chadwick. I told her I couldn't withhold information from the police, and she should call you. She left. And then I called to tell you and left a message..."

But I hadn't left any details. *Genius.* I studied my damp sneakers.

Jason closed his eyes, sighed, and hung his head, his hands on his slim hips. "She didn't call. Tell me more about this goblet."

I told him everything. "I know I'll get it back from Herb sooner or later. It's just... aggravating," I finished lamely. My excuse for coming here seemed like just that—an excuse, and a bad one.

"Why haven't you gone to look at the files in the warehouse? There may be info on the goblet there."

"I've been avoiding it. Everyone just assumes I'm going to accept the donation. They're certain I'll start a new, bigger, better paranormal museum somewhere else. I feel like I'm being railroaded."

"Like you were with the original paranormal museum?"

I opened my mouth. But instead of speaking, I drew in a long breath then exhaled. Jason wasn't chewing me out like I deserved. In the middle of a murder investigation, he was trying to help me out of my self-doubt.

My breath hitched, my throat thickening. He was an amazing man—better than I deserved. And it was time I cowgirled up. "Yeah."

"Did Chadwick know where the goblet was stored?"

I jammed my hands into the pockets of my hoodie. "What do you mean?"

His gold flecked eyes were serious. "I mean, you didn't know the goblet was in the Clarke collection until you went into that warehouse. The goblet's probably a side issue, tangential to the case. But maybe Chadwick talked to Clayton about it. Maybe he stopped by the warehouse to see it."

"I'll find out." Why hadn't I thought of that earlier?

But did the goblet matter? I shook my head. When you didn't know the truth, everything mattered.

"Let me know what you learn." He nodded and moved across the lawn toward Laurel and Bob.

Taking that as a dismissal, I returned to my pickup. I drove to the museum on autopilot and parked in the brick alley behind it.

Slowly, I walked through the tearoom's shared hallway. Part of me hoped to catch Adele in a lull. I was hoping for... What? A sympathetic ear? Absolution?

But her tearoom was hopping. The white-clothed tables were full, the chatter of diners a cheerful hum.

I pressed the spine on the bookcase. Adele whisked food to a table. The hidden door pivoted inward, and I walked into the museum. It smelled of fresh paint.

Something screeched, and I winced. Dieter's head popped up from behind a shelf. His hair stood in wild, dusty spikes. "Hey, perfect timing. I'm done." He rose and swiveled the shelf into place. "You can open tomorrow." He brushed his hands off, leaving smears on his paint-stained coveralls.

"Great," I said. "Thanks."

"You okay?" He rested his long, bronzed arm on the shelf. His brown eyes were unnaturally serious. Or maybe not so unnaturally. Marriage to Adele seemed to have steadied him.

"Yeah," I said. "Yeah, I'm fine. There's just a lot to do."

"Well, if you need any help, let me know." He bent and picked up his toolbox then ambled past me and into the tearoom. The bookcase swung shut behind him.

GD raised his head from the glass counter and meowed.

"Rea's dead," I told the cat. "And the police think Belle may be involved." The black cat sneezed.

"I don't know what to think either." Aside from the fact I hadn't acted quickly enough, hadn't told Jason enough. I walked behind the counter and pulled the cheap laptop I kept there from beneath it.

I booted it up and checked our online store. We had several orders for t-shirts, hoodies, and books on the occult. Filling orders was exactly the sort of mindless distraction I needed. I turned off my brain and packed bubble-envelopes and boxes.

Someone knocked on the front door, and I glanced at it. Looking grim, Price Keegan, his dress shirt open at the collar, loomed on the other side of the glass. He lifted one bony hand in a half-hearted wave. His fine, white shirt sleeves were rolled to his elbows.

I walked around the counter and unlocked the door. The bell above it jangled as I let him inside, surprised he wasn't wearing a jacket.

"What can I do for you?" I asked the vineyard owner.

Beneath his brown eyes, the skin was the color of a bruise. He combed a hand through his dark hair, glittering with mist. "Have you heard about Rea Bobberson?"

I nodded, a hard lump forming in my throat. "Yes. I found the body."

"Oh. Damn. I'm sorry." Price studied the checkerboard floor, then looked up to meet my gaze. "Why were you at her house?"

"I was looking for information on your brother's research." I shut the door behind him.

His mouth flattened. "Because they were seeing each other."

"You knew?" I asked, surprised.

"I think everyone knew. Her husband certainly did."

I gaped. "What?" Bob had *known*?

"Chadwick loved her. It was obvious, to me at least. I don't know if it meant as much to Rea though. I warned him he'd get hurt. He told me to stay out of it, that Bob knew and wasn't going to do anything to him. That wasn't what I'd meant when I said he'd get hurt," he said brokenly.

Bracing one shoulder against the old-fashioned register, I folded my arms. "Bob *knew*?"

"My brother told me Bob had confronted him." He jammed his hands into the pockets of his expensive-looking slacks and hunched his shoulders. "Chadwick said... he said Bob cried."

The scene flashed unwillingly into my overimaginative brain. "Oh," I said quietly.

Price looked toward the bronze skull on its pedestal. "I didn't want to say anything about it. With Chadwick dead, I thought maybe Rea and Bob could sort things out."

The story felt... true. We were silent a long moment. I swallowed. "You didn't think Bob might have killed Chadwick?" I asked. "And now his wife?"

"Bob Bobberson?" He shook his head. "Are you kidding me? He doesn't have it in him. At least, I didn't think he did. And it didn't seem worth revealing my brother's secret. Chadwick wouldn't have wanted that."

I didn't think so either. But my belief wasn't enough. The police needed evidence.

"So why are you telling me now?" A flash of anger heated my cheeks. I'd gone through this before with Rea. She'd ignored my advice and died. I was done with being everyone's confessor. And I'd be sure to tell Jason about this—in a detailed message, if necessary. "You need to tell the police."

He sighed and showed me his palms. "I know."

"How do you know Bob?"

"He and Rea are in the wine club. And I'm telling you because... you're interested."

"So are the police."

"Yeah." He studied his polished black shoes. "But you're different. It's their job. You *want* to know. So do I. My brother and I didn't always get along, but he was still my brother."

"You're assuming a lot about me."

A motorcycle roared past on the street outside. Involuntarily, I glanced out the front window. But it was a motorcycle I didn't recognize.

"You came to me with your friend to ask about his fiancée," Price said. "And Penny told me more about you. She spoke highly of you. Did you find my brother's research?"

"No. As far as I know, his laptop is still AWOL. What did his laptop bag look like?"

"He was so proud of it." The corners of his mouth turned downward. "A top-of-the-line laptop backpack, complete with a charging cable. Black, of course."

"When was the last time you saw your brother? Not including at Mrs. Grandall's party."

"It was about a week before. He came to the winery, and we had a few glasses. It was after hours. I think he'd just left Rea—not broken up with her, left a, er, date. He was full of himself. Chadwick treated me to one of his California history lectures. It was the usual story, how unfair the gold rush had been to everyone who'd come before—the natives, the Spaniards, even John Sutter. The gold rush ruined him."

I nodded. John Sutter was a Swiss national who'd moved to the California territory and built a fort. Generous to a fault, he let the newcomers walk all over him, stealing his supplies.

"I understand your brother was researching Vincenzo Benedetto?" I asked.

"Yeah. I think that was just to get in good with Mrs. Grandall. He was hoping she'd fund his research."

"Did Chadwick mention anything about the Benedetto goblet?" I asked.

"The what?"

And that was a *no*. "Never mind."

"What happened with Rea?"

I shook my head. "I found her at her house. She was dead at the bottom of the stairs. I don't think the police want me to say any more." Jason wouldn't have approved of me saying even that much.

"Was Bob there?" he asked.

"He came later, after the police arrived."

"I wasn't wrong to keep my brother's affair quiet. Bob didn't do this." His brown eyes held a pleading look. "You see that, right?"

I nodded. I saw that he wanted to believe it. He wanted to believe his silence hadn't caused his brother's death. But I didn't trust any of it. Not telling the police about the affair to protect Bob and Rea? It made no sense.

Maybe Price had come to me for absolution. If so, he wasn't the only one looking for that. Or maybe he'd come to me to learn what I knew.

chapter eighteen

I LIKE TO THINK I learn from my mistakes. So after Price left the museum, I called Jason.

"I can't tell you where we are in the investigation," he said before I could speak.

I leaned against the counter. Watery afternoon sunlight streamed through the front windows and gleamed greasily off the glass. "Chadwick's brother, Price just stopped by the museum," I said.

GD sniffed my elbow, and absently, I reached behind me to pet the black cat. Naturally, he bit me. I rubbed my hand and winced. So much for learning from my mistakes.

"What did he want?" Jason asked cautiously.

I checked my hand. At least no skin was broken. The cat seemed to know exactly how much pressure to apply without crossing the line. "I think he wanted to let me know that his brother was having an affair with Rea."

"We already knew that."

"And that her husband knew." The tip jar was too close to the counter's edge, and I shifted it closer to the old-fashioned cash register.

"Bob knew? That's... interesting," Jason said. "How could Price be sure?"

"He said his brother told him Bob confronted him about it."

He grunted. "Which we only have Price's word for."

It could all be a lie. Price might have told me in the hopes of making Bob a better suspect. That might take the heat off Price. "I told him to contact the police about it."

Jason laughed shortly. "Thanks. I'd ask why he decided to confide in you, but I can guess the answer. Does he know about our relationship?"

"I don't know. I didn't mention it."

Someone rapped on the museum's front door, and I glanced over my shoulder. My mother, Cora, and a hatchet-faced woman named Eliza stared through the window. "I've got to go," I said. "My mom's here."

"I'll see you tonight."

My heart warmed. Jason couldn't be too mad at me if our date was still on. "Bye."

I hung up and opened the door, the bell above it jingling. "What brings Ladies Aid to the museum?"

Eliza sniffed and brushed an invisible fleck of something off her navy parka. "It wasn't my idea."

"But we're so glad you were able to come with us." Cora smiled at the woman and adjusted the folds of her purple cloak.

Eliza had once been president of Ladies Aid. In a hostile takeover, Cora and my mother had become the new co-presidents. Eliza had neither forgiven nor forgotten.

"Have you found the Benedetto goblet yet?" Eliza asked me.

"Herb's taking care of it for now." I shut the door behind them.

"In other words," Eliza said, "no."

"He seems to think the goblet's cursed," I said, ignoring the implied criticism.

"So we've heard," my mother said. She was bundled in an elegant ivory knee-length coat over jeans and a denim top. "But that's not why we're here. We're interested in its retrieval, of course, but we have full confidence in you on that score. We're here about the plans for the new museum."

I stiffened. I didn't need them on my back. "I still haven't officially accepted the donation."

"Change is hard." Cora took my hand and patted it. "You've done so much with this little place. It must be difficult to think of letting it go. I confess, it will be strange not to see it on Main Street anymore."

"It's an eyesore," Eliza said.

"It lures tourists from the vineyards to the shops and restaurants downtown." My mother's voice sounded weary. I suspected this was a familiar argument.

"And with the Wok and Bowl closing..." Cora trailed off. "So much change."

I sucked in a breath, a heavy feeling settling in my stomach. "Wait," I said. "What? The Wok and Bowl is shutting down?"

True, I was more likely to drop a bowling ball on my toes than knock over any pins. But the Wok and Bowl was a San Benedetto institution. And their Chinese food was really good.

"The owners are retiring," Cora said. "No one wants a bowling alley anymore. I hear a developer made an offer they couldn't refuse."

"They'll knock it down and build something mixed use that looks like every other mixed use building in every other town." Eliza wrinkled her nose as if she'd smelled something distasteful.

I gaped at the trio. No more Wok and Bowl? I couldn't believe it. Next thing they'd be doing was pave over the vineyards.

My mother adjusted her squash blossom necklace. "Mrs. Butterson owns a vacant building just a few blocks from here. It's off Main Street, but it's close enough to downtown to work for your museum."

"Which one?" I asked in spite of myself.

"You know it," my mother said. "It used to hold a Swedish furniture store."

"Are you kidding me?" Sure, it was big enough. Maybe. But it was a brutalist structure built in the 1970s, when people should have known better. "That place is a pit."

GD slunk toward us. The black cat's belly was low to the ground, his tail lashing.

"I'm sure it can be modernized," my mother said.

"But this is an old collection," I said. "Antiques. Bad modern doesn't fit the vibe."

"Vibe? It's a paranormal museum," Eliza said. "Your vibe is bizarre."

"My museum is charming." I motioned to the black crown molding. "I don't want to go full creeptastic. It's been done. There are freaky-deaky paranormal museums all over the country. Mine may be weird, but it's weird-cute. That building isn't."

GD raised a paw. The cat batted the hem of Cora's purple cloak.

"She does have a point," Cora murmured. "Her museum has always been more educational than hair-raising."

"Thank you," I said. GD meowed an agreement.

"Well you have to find *somewhere* bigger," my mother said. "Besides, this place is falling apart." She nodded to the freshly painted wall.

I rolled my eyes. Of *course* she'd heard about the flood. Ladies Aid knew everything. I was surprised they hadn't solved the murders yet themselves.

As if she could read my mind, my mother said, "I heard you found poor Rea Bobberson's body."

"Yeah," I said heavily.

"How'd she die?" Eliza asked.

"Ah..." Jason wouldn't want me to blab. On the other hand, I didn't actually know for *certain* how she'd died. Maybe she was in the habit of wearing green cords like a scarf. "She was at the bottom of the stairs."

"Pushed, no doubt," Eliza said.

"I heard she was strangled with a curtain cord," Cora said brightly.

I blinked. Was that what it had been? "Where'd you hear that?"

"Oh," Cora said, "here and there. You know how it is. People talk."

My neck tightened. Then the SBPD had a leak, because I hadn't said anything about that green cord. "Well, thanks for stopping by."

But the ladies didn't take the hint. My mother folded her arms over her long, ivory coat. "No more shillyshallying. What are your plans regarding the museum?"

Oh, crud. What were my plans? "My plans...are..." *Plans, plans, plans.* "...to have a sit down with Clayton and get a better sense of the size and scope of his collection."

"When?" my mother asked.

"I was just going to call and set an appointment." I plucked my cellphone off the counter.

"Excellent. Let us know how it goes," my mother said. She turned and exited the museum. The other two women followed.

Since they'd probably find out if I didn't do it, I called Clayton. To my great regret, he answered.

He agreed to meet me at the warehouse that night. "I've made an extra set of keys for you. I'll give them to you tonight."

"Thanks," I said, unenthusiastic.

We said our goodbyes, and I flipped the sign in the window to OPEN. I'd planned on keeping the museum closed all day, but what the heck?

A few people did wander in. No one complained about the paint smell, but it was giving me a headache.

At six, I closed up, took two aspirin, and drove to the big corrugated-metal warehouse. Clayton's car sat outside.

I walked to the door. It stood ajar, beery light from within knifing across the pavement. I pushed the door wider. "Clayton?"

Considering his paranormal phobia, I was surprised he'd gone inside the warehouse without me.

Surprised and a little worried.

Skin prickling, I stepped into the warehouse. Something rustled above me, and I looked into the high rafters. A pigeon landed on one of the hanging industrial lights. The metal lamp swayed. Its conical light skimmed like a searchlight across the concrete aisle.

"Clayton?" I moved down the row of caged carrels. The door to one of the cages stood open. Closed metal bookcases with windowed doors filled the room.

"Clayton?" I whispered. Swallowing, I walked inside.

The cases were about as tall as I was. They hummed faintly.

I glanced in their windows as I walked down the aisles of bookcases. The cases were full of old books, some leather-bound.

One book that looked to be from the middle ages lay open on a stand inside a case. Its pages flamed with color—a naked man and woman surrounded by the symbols of the zodiac.

I sucked in a breath. *Good God*. The book was gorgeous. And old. And likely very, very valuable.

And it might be mine. Supernatural avarice fizzed through my veins.

"Hey."

I squeaked and leapt away from the case, my arm banging into the one behind it.

Clayton laughed sheepishly. "Sorry. I didn't mean to startle you."

"I thought..." I pressed a hand to my wildly beating heart. "Never mind what I thought. Thanks for meeting me. I was hoping to get a look at some of the documentation on the objects." I motioned around the room. "Specifically, the Benedetto goblet."

He shook his head. "Everyone's interested in that. That poor man who was killed even asked me about it."

Then Jason had been right. And he was certainly right about the limits to amateur detecting. But I couldn't help myself. "Chadwick?" I asked breathlessly. "When? What'd you tell him?"

"It was three weeks ago. I brought him here, to the warehouse. He photographed the goblet and read up on its provenance."

"Read up on it? The provenance document is here?"

He nodded.

"I'd like to see that document," I said.

"Certainly." He led me into a small office and walked to a wooden file cabinet. Pulling it open, he said, "You're lucky. It took me a lot longer to find the document for Chadwick. But now I know where to lay my hands on it."

He withdrew a slim manila folder from the cabinet, glanced inside, and passed it to me. "It's not much," he said.

I opened the folder.

"You can sit down, if you like." He motioned toward a rolltop desk and captain's chair in front of it.

"Thanks." I sat.

He switched on a desk lamp with a green-glass shade and shifted an open wooden box aside. He made to close its lid on a small, antique gun nestled atop the box's red velvet lining. Beside the tiny gun lay a stake and mallet, bottle and Bible.

I gasped. "Hold on," I said. "Is that a vampire hunter's kit?"

He shrugged. "My Dad had three. This is from the 1800s, I think."

Three? Astonished, I shook myself then opened the folder. There was only one typed page inside, with a signed invoice attached. I flipped it over, then read the front.

SIPHON GLASS FROM CATALONIA. PREVIOUSLY IN THE COLLECTION OF BERTRAM GRANDALL. PURCHASED FOR ONE THOUSAND, FIVE HUNDRED DOLLARS ON OCTOBER 19, 1985.

The clear glass goblet once belonged to Vincenzo Benedetto and passed on to his heir, Marcus Benedetto, then to his heir Sarah Grandall, then to Jonathan Grandall, and finally to Betram. Inside its goblet are what remains of a "surprise" siphon apparatus. This straw-like device would allow a stream of liquid to spurt through a hole in one of the rings on the goblet's hollow sphere between the bowl of the goblet and its foot, surprising unwary drinkers.

The famed Benedetto goblet was the equivalent of a dribble glass? *Figures.* I frowned. "It's from Catalonia? I thought Vincenzo was Italian, not Spanish."

Clayton shrugged. "There's no reason he couldn't have bought a Catalonian gag goblet. There *was* international commerce back then, and Spain wasn't far from Italy."

"Of course, you're right. I don't suppose it would have any impact on why it's haunted." I flipped the stapled invoice over. "Speaking of which, there's no mention here of *why* it's haunted."

"It's on the other page."

"What other page?" I picked up the paper. "There's nothing else in this file."

"But of course there is." He took the folder from my hands. "This is…" His forehead puckered. "But there was at least one other sheet of paper in here. It was handwritten, yellowing. I saw it."

I glanced around the concrete floor. "Could it have fallen out?"

We searched the office but couldn't find the paper. Clayton even pulled out the other folders in the cabinet, to no avail.

"He took it," Clayton fumed. "Chadwick took it. But why?"

The skin on my arms pebbled. *Why indeed?*

chapter nineteen

"CHADWICK STOLE A DOCUMENT from your museum?" Jason asked. His charcoal suit jacket lay neatly folded over the back of the chair between us. He'd flung his crimson tie over one shoulder to keep it out of the egg drop soup.

I set my chopsticks on the linoleum table. The noise of balls striking pins clattered through the bowling alley. "It's not my museum. It's not even my stuff yet. I haven't officially accepted the donation."

Jason cocked an eyebrow. He tilted his dark head.

"Okay," I admitted, "I *am* going to accept it. Clayton had a 19th century vampire hunter's kit just lying around. How can I not accept that?"

He grinned. "You claim to be a paranormal agnostic, but you love this stuff."

"I am an agnostic, *and* I love this stuff. It's history, even if it's weird history. And it's an important part of the human experience. And no, I'm not just saying that to sell tickets to my museum. Magic and the paranormal have always been a part of human history. There's a reason for that." I wasn't sure what that reason was, but there *had* to be a reason.

More importantly, Jason had forgiven me my sins, and relief slackened my muscles. I hoped I deserved it. I hoped I deserved *him*.

Jason speared a piece of Mongolian beef. "Does Clayton have any idea what was on that page?"

"Only that it has to do with the Benedetto goblet."

"Which we know Chadwick was researching."

"But why steal the page? He could have just taken a picture of it with his phone. And Chadwick was trying to be a legit researcher, I think. I mean, he was going for his PhD. You don't do that by stealing research."

"It is odd." Jason laid his hand atop mine, and my skin tingled at the contact. "I'll keep an eye out for the document. We'll get it back."

We. Soft warmth filled my chest. Jason and I were best when we were working together. "That's not what I'm really worried about." Though the missing page did bother me. "Is there any word on Belle?"

"No." He shook his head. "And that's all I can tell you."

"I know," I said, rueful. "I'm sorry I asked." So why *had* I asked? Why couldn't I keep my mouth shut?

Jason smiled slightly. "Don't be sorry. I love that you're the kind of person who cares. So what are you going to do with the museum now that it's expanding?"

I sat back in the red chair. "There's so much. Create a non-profit, find a new location." My voice cracked on the last syllable. "I hate losing my museum on Main Street. Yes, it's too small. It's been getting too small for a while now. But... it's *way* too small for the new collection. Then again, what if the new place is too big for the number of customers?"

Bowling pins crashed, and there was a cheer. I glanced at the group of women in pink bowling shirts.

"What do you mean?" he asked.

I refocused on Jason. "What if I expand, but I have the same amount of people coming to the new museum? It may be a nonprofit, but I'll still have to pay bills. Not to mention paying myself. Paranormal museums are popping up all over the country. How will this one be different?"

"I thought you were sticking with having more of a historical flavor. Aren't you going for more charm than gross-out?"

Pleasure fizzed in my chest. At least *someone* listened to me. "Yes, that. And I certainly can. Clayton's father has an amazing collection. I wouldn't be surprised if we get real PhD students coming in to do research."

"You don't think Chadwick was a real PhD student?"

I shook my head. "No, I didn't mean that." I shifted in my chair. But what *had* I meant? "I'm just saying, I don't know if charm and history are enough. I need to do something really special to pull people in."

The owner of the Wok and Bowl, Arthur Chang, approached our table. He smiled, the fine lines deepening around his brown eyes. "How's your meal?"

Arthur was a slender man with thinning hair. He wore tan slacks. His matching Cuban-style bowling shirt sported two wide white stripes down the front.

"It's excellent, as usual," Jason said. "But I hear you're closing down."

Arthur's smile morphed into a grimace. "Retirement. It's time. And the kids don't want this place."

"What are you going to do with it?" Jason looked around the high-ceilinged alley.

"I've got an offer from a developer," the older man said. "They've shown me their plans. Mixed use. They can cram a hundred housing units into this space."

I sighed. Another new development. Eliza had been right. It likely *would* look like every other new development. "I'm sorry to see the Wok and Bowl go," I said. "It's a San Benedetto institution."

"Everything comes to an end," Arthur said. "And I hear your museum is in for some changes too. I liked it. It's quirky and not too scary for the kids. Just right. But everything changes."

"Yeah," I said heavily. "I wish there was a way I could keep my old museum and start a new one. But it's just not realistic..." I trailed off.

The two men kept talking. I mentally lunged for the brainstorm that had come and gone. But the notion had vanished.

I shook my head. If it was a good idea, it would come back. I hoped.

The next morning, before the museum opened, I met Harper in her office at the Town Hall. She unrolled a map on top of the conference room table.

Morning sunlight knifed through the miniblinds and angled across the map. Several properties had been highlighted in yellow.

"This is everything that's up for sale within two miles of the town center." My friend smoothed the front of her coffee-colored turtleneck. "The bad news is, there's only one building available with more than five-thousand square feet."

"The old furniture store," I said, glum. That building was just so... soulless.

"The old furniture store." Harper braced one fist on the table and the other on her hip. "Honestly, I think it's a great location. The building's in decent condition. You'll need to do some work on it, but that would be true of anywhere you moved."

There was a knock on the glass door. A silver-haired woman in cat's-eye spectacles and a tweed skirt suit walked inside. Her low heels were silent on the thin, adobe-colored carpet. "Sorry to interrupt. I found the plans for that furniture store."

"This is our archivist," Harper said. "Mrs. Pruett."

"Archivist?" I asked. "As in historical?"

"Yes," the older woman said. "Our files aren't as glamorous as the Historical Association's. But we like to keep them in good order."

"I don't suppose Chadwick Keegan ever stopped by?" I asked. It was a shot in the dark. But what the heck?

"That poor boy who was killed?" Her brown eyes widened behind her glasses. "Yes, he was here two weeks ago, looking through our files."

"Really?" I asked, excited. "Which files?"

"Old maps from early San Benedetto days."

"Any maps in particular?" I asked.

"The original rancho that Vincenzo Benedetto bought for a song. Four thousand acres for a dollar an acre."

If he'd been researching Vincenzo and the goblet, there was nothing odd or unusual about wanting to see his property map. "Was a dollar an acre a good deal back then?" I asked.

The archivist laughed. "Oh, yes. If poor Salvador's widow hadn't been so eager to return to Spain, he never would have gotten all that land so cheaply."

"What happened to Salvador?" I asked. If Anne was right, he'd been the real first vineyard owner in the area. But he who lives longest gets the credit. Not that it mattered to Vincenzo or Salvador anymore.

"Farming accident," the archivist said. "They were common in those days. Well, I'll leave you two ladies to it." The older woman exited the room.

Harper rolled up the oversized map. "Want to take a look at that old furniture store? I've got the keys."

I could think of a dozen things I'd rather be doing, starting with clipping my toenails. "Um, not right now. It's Friday. I've got to open the museum."

"What about after work?"

"I'm helping Harriet with the final setup for the Mud Run."

"But it's our ladies night at the brewery," she said.

"And busy community-minded women need to make sacrifices," I joked, zipping up my hoodie.

"You sound like your mother."

I shuddered. "Bite your tongue."

Harriet bundled up a stack of race cards for the runners to wear. A quarter moon hung low in the sky. Its reflection rippled briefly in the nearby mud pit and then vanished as if devoured by the murky water.

Involuntarily, I glanced skyward to assure myself it had only disappeared behind a cloud. The moon would come back, unlike the past, unlike all the beautiful and not-so-beautiful parts of San Benedetto that were being torn down.

The Historical Association director looked around the wide, dirt track. "Oh, no."

"What's wrong?" I asked.

"I left the box of t-shirts back by the Z-wall."

"I'll go and get them," I said. I hadn't been much help so far, mainly providing Harriet someone to talk to as I trekked after her. By fetching and carrying, at least I could provide *some* value tonight.

The older woman shot me a relieved smile. "Thank you, dear. I'll see you in the parking area."

I walked down the dark track and passed a few volunteers going in the opposite direction. The earthmoving equipment was gone. The track was done. The signs were up. We were as ready as we'd ever be for tomorrow's race.

At the Z-shaped climbing wall, I turned on my phone's light and scanned the ground. A cardboard box lay near the mud pit. I hefted it up. It was heavier than I'd expected, and I was glad I was hauling it instead of Harriet.

An owl hooted from a nearby tree. Uneasy, I looked around the dark track. I was alone, and there were no wild animals to worry about here. Still, I walked more loudly as I trekked down the tree-lined trail toward the parking lot.

A branch cracked in the undergrowth. Pivoting, I aimed my phone's light in that direction. The pale beam bounced jerkily, illuminating a tangle of branches, washed of color.

No pale eyes gleamed in the beam of light. No fangs flashed. No tail lashed.

Paranoid, paranoid, paranoid. Releasing a breath, I kept walking.

Bushes rustled. The back of my neck prickled, but I kept walking. I have a big imagination. It's served me well at my work, but it's gotten the better of me in the past. The rustling had to be a bird. A big cat or coyote wouldn't be making that much noise.

It's only a bird. Or a squirrel. Or... a rattlesnake.

The branches exploded in a shower of dried leaves. I gasped, jumped, and swiveled to face the dark shape lunging from the bracken.

I yelped and dropped the box. And I just stood there.

chapter twenty

IT TOOK AN EMBARRASSINGLY long moment to realize he—and it was definitely a he—was running at *me*. I mean, when someone tumbles out of the bushes at night, my first instinct isn't that I'm under attack. It's to empathize with their unexpected pratfall.

It took too long for me to register the black gaiter covering most of his face. It took too long to see the hoodie zipped to his chin. It took too long to notice his hood was up, though the night was warm.

The man hurtled forward, and I stood gaping.

The t-shirts saved me. He tripped over the box I'd dropped and sprawled on the earthen track with a curse.

The curse jolted me. I turned and bolted.

There was a grunt. Too quickly, footsteps pounded behind me.

Heart banging in my chest, I hurdled a hay bale, pale in the moonlight. I veered around a tire course, my pursuer's steps growing ever closer.

There was a masculine shout and another thud. My follower had tripped over something else.

So at least I had one thing going for me. He was clumsy. Or he didn't know the course as well as I did. I knew to run around the logs instead of trying to hop over them.

I kept running, widening the distance between us. But I didn't get long to revel in my advantage. Soon he was closing on me again.

A stitch spearing my side, I sprinted up a short, steep hill. At its top stood a gallows-like construction. A knotted rope hung from the cross bar, its end hooked to the post. My breath rasped.

On the other side of the rise would be a mud pit. Runners could either slither down the hill and through the mud or swing across the watery barrier, the latter approach being faster. I needed faster.

At the top, I grabbed the rope. Moonlight glittered on the rectangular pool below. My hands shook as I unhooked the rope. It slipped from my gasp, swinging outward and away without me.

Something whispered against the back of my hoodie. With an incoherent shout, I jumped. By some miracle, I managed to grab the loose rope. I swung, arcing over the dark water.

My pursuer skidded down the bank and bolted along the side of the pool. Time slowed, in that funny way it does when you're sure you're about to die.

Because my swing hadn't gained me much advantage after all. I hadn't jumped hard or fast enough. My momentum was ebbing, the far edge of the pool growing closer ever more slowly.

A moan escaped my throat. I wouldn't make it to the other side. I'd land in the water, and then I'd be trapped. He'd catch me. I gripped the rope more tightly.

The rope's swing reached its apogee six feet from the opposite edge. My hands were hot and warm on the rough rope, my throat dry, my muscles tight and corded. The air smelled sweet, like drying herbs. The moon was a crooked scimitar on the dark water, and my shadow a furious, twisted huddle.

And then I swung backward.

My chest hardened. I wasn't going to go down without a fight. I'd scratch and claw and make sure there was plenty of DNA beneath my fingernails, preferably from his eyeballs.

My pursuer stopped to watch me swing toward the gallows. The man turned and raced back to the hill.

I swung closer. The shoulder of earth rose in front of me. I stuck out one leg to stop myself. My foot rebounded off the hillside with a jerk, and my hands slipped on the rough rope.

I squeaked. Looping the rope around one of my legs, I fought to hold on.

I swung out again, but even slower this time. The rope stopped a good seven feet from the edge of the pool before returning the way it had come.

I dared a glance at the man. He stood beside the mound, his hands on his hips.

"I'm not letting go," I shouted, arcing towards the low hillside. "I can hang here all night." My voice cracked, giving away the lie.

Anyone who knew me would have laughed at my claim. I'd never managed rope climbing in gym class. But fear can provide great inspiration. Also, with the rope hooked around my leg, it took a good bit of my weight off.

All that swinging was making me a little sick though. I closed my eyes to still my stomach.

When I opened them, the man was gone. The rope wobbled to a halt. I dangled above the center of the pool.

But had the man really left?

I clung so tight to the rope I was practically wrapped around myself. My leg ached where the rope bit into my jeans. My palms were damp and hot despite the chill night air. My arms trembled with the strain.

Harriet would be wondering what happened to me. She might come to look. But she'd be even less of a match for whoever'd been hunting me than I was. *Would* she come looking for me? Or would some nice, strong man volunteer to do it for her?

My hands slipped a fraction of an inch, and my heart jumped into my throat. I couldn't stay glued to this rope forever. But if the man was nearby, if he heard the splash...

I swallowed. I'd have to risk it. I lifted my leg, releasing the rope wound around my calf. *Just let g—*

My hands spasmed. I hit the freezing water, remembering to relax my legs at the last second because the pit wasn't all that deep.

My feet touched bottom, and I stumbled backward. Flailing, I only barely managed to keep my head above the water.

Shivering, I lurched to standing. Footsteps padded toward me, and my heart gripped. He was coming back.

Frantic, I thrashed through the water and braced my hands on the pit's rough dirt edge. A pair of well-shod shoes stepped smartly to the side of the pit. I gasped and splashed backward.

Jason looked down and arched a brow. "Testing the course?"

"N-n-no." My teeth chattered. "There was a man in black. With a mask. He chased me."

"Where?" his voice razored.

I pointed toward the hillside. Jason darted over the hill and vanished.

I clambered from the pit. Dripping, I stood for a moment and considered my options.

Then I sloshed back to the point in the trail where I'd dropped the t-shirts and started to extricate myself from my hoodie and paranormal museum tee. My tops fought back, unwilling to relinquish their freezing grips.

Finally I wrestled free and put on a dry Mud Run t-shirt. Then I put on another.

Jason rejoined me as I finished gathering up the shirts scattered along the trail. "No luck," he said.

That much was obvious. If he'd caught the guy, my pursuer would be in handcuffs. I brushed dirt off the last of the shirts and jammed it back into the box.

Jason extended his arms. "I'll carry those. Harriet told me you'd gone looking for these and hadn't come back."

I gave him the box. "H-Harriet's a g-good egg."

He set down the shirts, shrugged out of his suit jacket, and slung it over my shoulders. "You're freezing."

I wanted to hug him. But I was also muddy, and now so was his jacket, so I settled for blowing him a kiss. We started off toward the parking lot.

"What did this guy look like?" he asked.

I shook my head. "I didn't get a good look. I couldn't even tell you his height. He was wearing an over-sized hoodie, and it's dark. Sorry."

"Don't be sorry. You're safe. That's what counts." Jason hesitated. "I'd ask if you were sure you were being chased, but you say he was wearing a mask?"

"His face was covered by something. I don't know what, but the fabric was dark too."

Jason slung his free arm around my shoulder and rubbed my arm. But it was my chest that heated. If he didn't care I was wet and filthy... I leaned closer, grateful for his warmth.

He sighed. "I suppose there's no use asking why someone would be chasing you. How many suspects have you and Mason been harassing?"

"I wouldn't say harassing," I said loftily.

"No, I guess you wouldn't." His tone hardened. "I'll have a word with Mason."

"Why?"

"Because he's put you in danger. He's not thinking."

I stopped short. Mason hadn't done anything. "We don't know that. This could be about the paper Chadwick stole from my collection."

He arched a brow. "*Your* collection?"

"I told you I was accepting it. I just need to figure out the details." And there were a lot of details. I ruminated on them as we trekked back to the parking lot. They were more comfortable to think about than the guy who'd been chasing me.

The driver's door to Harriet's gold Mazda hatchback opened. She stepped from the small car. "There you are. I was getting wor—" Her mouth formed an O. "What happened?"

"I had an accident," I said, my shoulders drawing upward. "Sorry. I took two of the t-shirts. And some are a little, ah, dirty."

"We have plenty," she said, studying me. "You must be freezing. Go home. Get dry."

I nodded, then paused. Harriet was no frail Edwardian lady to be protected from unpleasantness. She might know something. "Actually, it wasn't really an accident. Someone chased me."

"What?" The elderly director pressed a hand to her chest. "Who?"

"The man was wearing a mask," I said. "I think it might have something to do with Rea and Chadwick."

Jason cleared his throat.

"What a tragedy." Harriet lowered her head.

"Did you know they were having an affair?" I asked.

Her head jerked up. "What? Rea and Chadwick? No," she said explosively. "She was nearly twice his age."

"That doesn't stop some people," Jason said.

She fiddled with the chain that held her glasses. "No. No, I suppose it doesn't."

"You didn't have any idea something was going on between them?" I asked.

"No. But... they *were* rather close. I didn't think anything of it at the time, but I suppose it's possible there was more. You're sure they were having an affair?"

"Not a hundred percent," I said. Nothing was a hundred percent. "But I have it on good authority."

"They *were* working closely together," Harriet said. "Do you think the affair is what got them killed? Oh, but I can't believe it. Bob is such a *nice* man."

I wrapped my arms around myself and shivered. Because sometimes nice men did terrible things.

chapter twenty-one

I ALMOST SCREAMED WHEN the hot water hit my palms, red and raw from clinging to that rope. But I survived. And I stepped from the shower feeling marginally more human and loads warmer. I dressed quickly in a clean pair of jeans and a t-shirt and emerged into my tiny living area.

Jason sat on the blue sofa frowning at his phone. There was something comforting about the cramped apartment. Its distressed wood floors and nautical theme of soft blues, whites and grays were soothing.

The color scheme was my aunt's choice, not mine. But it was her garage apartment, and the rent was low. So though we were over a hundred miles from the Pacific, I wasn't about to complain about the shadow boxes with starfish and coral hanging from the white-washed walls. Or about the old mariner's equipment that worked as bookends. Or the telescope in its battered leather case. The gleaming sextant. The dusty captain's hat.

I really needed to dust that hat. *Tomorrow.*

Jason looked up and grinned. "You clean up good." His suit jacket was slung over the back of the couch. His white shirt sleeves were rolled at the cuffs, exposing his dark, sinewy arms.

"Thanks." I smiled back. "I feel better."

He set the phone on the coffee table beside a basket of starfish and seashells. "Maybe you should tell me what's happened since yesterday."

"There's not much to tell," I said and sat beside him on the couch. "Or I would have told you sooner."

"Go on." He draped his arm over my shoulders.

I snuggled closer. "I found out Chadwick talked to the archivist at town hall a couple weeks back," I continued. "He was looking at old maps of San Benedetto."

Jason nodded. "Mrs. Pruett? I'll speak with her. What else?"

"Nothing else." My voice rose on the last word, and I cleared my throat. "Ladies Aid is on my back about getting the new museum going. Mrs. Grandall wants that goblet. Herb refuses to hand it over until it's *safe*, whatever that means."

"I meant about the murder."

Jason might not be able to talk about his investigation, but I owed it to him to tell him more about mine. I plucked a starfish from the basket and laid it on the coffee table beside his phone. "You don't see Mrs. Grandall as the killer then?" I asked, swiveling the starfish on the table. "Because she's *really* interested in that goblet."

"Not to be ageist here, but she couldn't have broken Chadwick's neck."

I winced. "That was how he was killed?" That mode of death did speak to a man as the murderer. And it was a man who'd been chasing me tonight. I shuddered.

"So that leaves Bob Bobberson, Dr. MacDuff, or Chadwick's brother, Price." I set out a turret snail shaped like a unicorn's horn, a sea scallop, and a sand dollar.

"The sand dollar's Price?" Jason asked.

"I'm going with the metaphor. Price. Dollars. Keeping it simple."

"Thanks," he said dryly.

"Price was at the party. He had means. He seems to have resented his brother—something about the winery. Chadwick didn't want to be involved in the family business, but he *did* want to collect the income. Now that he's dead, it's all Price's."

"And Bob's motive is jealousy. If he did know about the affair, he had every reason to want Chadwick dead. He could have argued with his wife afterward and strangled her."

"You think Bob killed his wife in the heat of the moment?" I nudged the turret snail toward him.

"He has no alibi. He says he was driving, trying to clear his head. Tell me again about the ACHA director, MacDuff."

My insides warmed. Jason was confiding in me, rules or no. And he was usually a stickler for rules.

I picked up the sea scallop. "MacDuff was also at the party. According to the administrative assistant, Chadwick wrote MacDuff's PhD dissertation. Getting a PhD was key to him staying on as director of the ACHA."

"And if anyone found out he didn't do his own work..." Jason shook his head. "But you got this from the admin assistant. She knows the truth. Does MacDuff know she knows?"

"No idea."

"We'll keep an eye on her and MacDuff. Why the turret snail for Bobberson?"

I sighed. "There's just something about him..." I shook my head, unable to put my finger on what it was. "I don't know."

Footsteps sounded on the steps outside.

Jason frowned. "Are you expecting someone?"

I tensed. "No." Though a pizza delivery man wouldn't be amiss right now. Alas, I'd have to have ordered a pizza first, and I hadn't.

Jason rose and walked to the door. Someone knocked, and he opened it.

Mason, in a black motorcycle jacket and denims stood framed in the doorway. "Sorry to interrupt. Is Maddie here?"

"Yeah." I rose, my gut knotting. "Has something happened?"

"In a way."

Jason folded his arms, the fabric of his dress shirt rustling. "And you came to Maddie's home instead of calling the police?"

My neighbor's expression hardened. "Maddie keeps me updated on what she's found," he said pointedly.

I stiffened. He'd made it sound like I'd been going behind Jason's back. And I hadn't been.

"You know why I can't tell you everything," Jason said.

"Yeah, and—" Mason exhaled sharply. "Can I come in?"

"Of course," I said, ignoring the tension. There wasn't much I could do to relieve it anyway.

Jason stepped aside, and Mason strode past him. Jason closed the door.

"What's going on?" I asked.

"There's money missing from my shop's safe."

"I'm taking it there was no sign of a break-in," Jason said. "Did Belle have the combination?"

Mason's jaw hardened. "Yes."

"And you only just discovered this?" Jason cocked his head, his gold-flecked eyes narrowing.

"I don't go into the safe that often. I got a call from Lulu. She runs the salon Belle rents a chair from. She told me there was money missing from her cash box."

"And Lulu called you?" I asked. "Why does she think Belle was responsible?"

Mason's mouth compressed. "She told me she's been suspicious of Belle for some time but hasn't been able to prove anything. And she didn't want to believe it."

"Suspicious of what?" I asked.

"Apparently cash has been going missing on a regular basis."

My insides twisted. *Belle, a thief?* Was it possible?

Jason rubbed his jaw. "And you had no idea?"

"Of course I had no idea," Mason exploded. "Do you think that's okay with me? That because I ride a bike I'm a criminal?"

"No," Jason said in a low voice. "I don't."

Mason paced in front of the low wall separating the living area from the kitchen. "What am I supposed to tell Jordan?"

"Belle hasn't reached out to you at all?" Jason asked.

Mason whirled to face him and glared. "Aside from reaching into my safe? No."

"And you don't know of any other connection between Belle and Chadwick?" Jason asked. "Aside from her cutting his hair?"

Mason cut a guilty glance at me. "No."

"How did you know Chadwick was her client?" I asked coolly. Because I didn't think Belle and Mason sat around the dinner table discussing her client lists.

"He talked to her about San Benedetto history when she was cutting his hair," Mason said. "Sometimes she'd tell me and Jordan about it. I think she liked knowing more old stories about the town than I did."

"Do you remember any of those stories?" I asked him.

"Sure, how Chuck got the money for his Chicken Shack that became the paranormal museum. The history of the old lady who owned the bowling alley that became the Wok and Bowl. And Vincenzo Benedetto wasn't the golden boy history remembers him as."

My breath caught. *Vincenzo again?* "How so?"

Mason shrugged. "Belle said he cheated the Spanish woman he bought his land from. And he had a violent streak. He ran down a man who'd crossed him with his horse and buggy. The man survived, but he walked with a limp the rest of his life. Does it matter?"

"Probably not," Jason said. "But it's good to be thorough."

But I wasn't so sure. I gnawed my lower lip. Maybe the past didn't really die. Because lately it seemed to have an odd tendency to bleed into the present.

"Were there any other stories you remember?" I jammed my hands into the front pockets of my jeans.

Mason looked at the distressed wood floor. "She told me Vincenzo was known for his good luck. He'd catch one lucky break after another. Though I think him getting that land for a steal sounded less like luck than ruthlessness."

"Wasn't that goblet supposed to bring good luck?" Jason asked. "Maybe that's the goblet connection."

I frowned. "That's what people seemed to think." My mother had certainly thought so. So why did Herb think the goblet was cursed?

"I'll send some men to your shop to fingerprint that safe," Jason said. "And I'll talk to Lulu at the salon tomorrow."

Mason nodded. He looked at me uncertainly, then strode to my front door.

"Someone attacked Maddie at the Mud Run track tonight," Jason said, voice hard. "Next time you have something to say, come to me."

Mason turned. "Attacked? Are you okay?"

"Chased," I said. "Not attacked. I'm fine." I jammed my raw hands into the front pockets of my jeans and repressed a wince.

Mason hesitated. "I'm sorry." He turned and left. His booted feet descended the stairs, and he was gone.

chapter twenty-two

A WOMAN IN SHORTS and a tank top leapt for the rope and Tarzaned across the mud pit. The crowd cheered. Jason shot me a pointed look.

"I *meant* to fall in," I muttered and folded my arms. Plus, the morning's racer had the advantage of bright sunshine *and* not being chased by a masked criminal.

He grinned and looped his arm over my shoulder. "Sure you did."

"I did!" Why didn't anyone believe me? I'd chosen to fall in after logically deducing it was my best option.

He kissed the top of my head. "I'm just glad you're safe. I'd be more glad if you'd stop sticking your nose into my investigations. But we both know that's not going to happen."

I pressed my hand to my breastbone. "All I want is to figure out what's up with the cursed goblet. I'm not interfering in your murder investigation."

"Uh, huh." His expression turned doubtful.

"And to find Belle," I amended. *Before something bad happened to her.* I swallowed.

I hoped I was being paranoid. But with Rea dead... Rea *must* have known something about the murder—or about what Chadwick had been up to. And that had gotten her killed.

Unless Rea's husband had committed the crimes. I shifted my weight.

"Isn't that Mrs. Grandall?" Jason asked.

My pulse jumped. Mrs. Grandall, a determined glint in her eye, made her way through the crowd toward us. If she hadn't looked so elegant in her red tracksuit and sneakers, I might have taken the white-haired lady for a Mud Run participant.

I looked around. "Ah, you know, you should talk to her," I said. "Without me. And I need to check on..."

I ducked away. And yes, I *was* being a coward. But I didn't need another grilling over that goblet. I glanced over my shoulder.

Jason had stopped Mrs. Grandall. Her wrinkled face creased with annoyance.

I smiled. *Thank you.*

I thudded into a solid body. "Oof."

Eliza's hatchet face glared up at me. "Watch where you're going." Her close-cut gray hair bristled.

"Sorry." I made to step around her.

She raised a thick finger. "Not so fast. Have you found that goblet yet?"

"Yes," I said. "Herb has it."

"In other words, you haven't."

"It's not as if Herb's going to sell it to the highest bidder. It's perfectly safe. Honestly, he just needs to remove the curse—"

Eliza's face tightened. "What curse? The Benedetto goblet brings good luck to the harvest. Haven't you done any research at all?"

"Yes, I—"

"There you are," an imperious feminine voice said.

My shoulders slumped. I forced a smile and turned. "Hello, Mrs. Grandall."

Her nostrils pinched. "The goblet. Do you have it?"

"She doesn't," Eliza said.

"Herb is my trusted collector," I said. "He's removing the curse before the goblet's put on display."

Eliza snorted. "It's not cursed."

Patience. I counted to three. "I've been doing research—"

"How?" Mrs. Grandall asked.

"I have my ways," I said, and her sharp blue eyes narrowed. "And there's a provenance for the goblet back at Clayton's warehouse," I continued hastily. "It turns out, the goblet's actually from Spain. That funny straw in it is so it can squirt wine at unsuspecting drinkers. It's basically a gag goblet."

Mrs. Grandall's expression turned glacial.

"I don't see how any of that gets you closer to retrieving the goblet," Eliza said. "Are you sure you're up to the task?"

"Of retrieving the goblet?" I asked. Someone jostled me from behind, and I edged sideways. "Sure," I said. "No problem. Herb's going to bring it back."

"I meant about managing this new, *real* museum," she continued.

"But... my museum's real," I said weakly.

Mrs. Grandall tugged down the hem of her zip-up jacket. "I suppose you've developed long-term policies and standards of care for the objects."

My stomach bottomed. "Policies?" *Standards of care?* I kept everything clean and dry.

There was a splash. The crowd roared.

"Policies regarding new acquisitions, loans, exhibitions, packing, security, and their storage?" Mrs. Grandall asked, her voice quick with impatience.

"Well, no, but—"

"Do any of the objects have special needs, like climate control?" Mrs. Grandall tugged up the zipper on her track suit.

I thought of those humming cabinets in the warehouse. Had they been dehumidifiers? "Ah..." I smoothed the front of my Mud Run sponsor t-shirt. My stomach rolled, my throat turning to sandpaper.

"And of course, you won't be displaying the entire collection at once," the white-haired lady continued. "Where and how will things be stored when they're not displayed? How will you access and transport them? Do you need access twenty-four/seven? How will you store the objects until they're displayed?"

"I, ah..." My head swam. None of these issues had come up with my paranormal museum in the past. It was a *paranormal museum.* If I had any cleaning questions about an object, I just asked Herb.

Eliza's lip curled.

"Do you even have a mission statement?" Mrs. Grandall continued. "A historic collection of that size, value, and specificity requires an experienced curation team."

Mission statement? Curation team? I clutched my arms to my chest.

But she was right. My current museum was more roadside attraction than serious institution. The collection Clayton was donating was a whole other level. I didn't know how to curate a real collection, an important collection.

There was another splash behind me. The crowd laughed and cheered.

I rallied. "I have Herb."

"Who appears to have stolen one of the most important artifacts," Eliza chimed in.

"It's fine," I said wildly. "It's all fine. I have to get back to the museum. Busy, busy Saturday." I pivoted and darted through a gap in the crowd, my heart beating faster than I liked.

My breath came in shallow gasps. Was I hyperventilating?

I pressed a hand to my forehead. Sweat had beaded on it.

This was silly. It was just stuff. I could manage it. And creating a non-profit, and managing more staff, and finding a bigger place and managing rent and...

Dammit. I *was* hyperventilating.

I said my goodbyes to Jason and returned to the museum before the Mud Run ended at eleven. But I didn't need to stick around to know it had been a success.

By eleven-thirty, visitors from the run were flooding the museum. The crowds continued through Sunday. I'd like to think Leo and I managed them with aplomb even if we didn't have a stupid mission statement.

But I couldn't help wondering how things would be different if I took on the new collection. Something heavy quivered in the pit of my stomach. Could I do the Clarke collection justice?

Monday, I returned to the closed museum to feed GD and package the recent orders that had come in online. That task complete, I took a stab at writing a mission statement.

I stared at my yellow pad. I drummed my pen on the glass counter. I studied the fog pressing against the window. *Mission statement, mission statement...*

GD watched from the haunted rocking chair in the corner. His absinthe eyes glittered, pitiless.

"I just need a few examples to get started," I told the black cat.

Turning to my laptop, I searched the internet for other museum mission statements. Unfortunately, the paranormal museums I found online didn't seem to have any. At least none that they'd posted.

"So I'm not alone, here," I said. But my museum wouldn't be like other paranormal museums. I needed to think bigger. I clicked to a fine arts museum.

We believe the power of art can ignite the imagination...

"Nope." I opened another museum's web page.

...encouraging and developing the study of the fine arts...

"Definitely not." Maybe I needed to go back, start smaller. I typed "how to write a mission statement for a museum" into the search engine.

Use your mission statement as a lens to communicate to your visitors about your works.

"Unhelpful," I snarled, and I shut the laptop. I'd work on the mission statement later.

Gathering up the boxes and thick envelopes, I took the packages to the post office and trudged to the back of a long line. A mural of old California decorated the area above the old-fashioned, arched windows. Miners trudged toward the beckoning hills. They led donkeys with one hand, pickaxes slung over their opposite shoulders. I shifted the packages in my arms and sympathized.

Finally, I reached the front window and shipped the packages. But I didn't go home to work on my mission statement. I drove through the mist to our local Historical Association.

The scent of lemon furniture polish hit me when I walked through the door. In the foyer, Harriet frowned at the stack of papers in her hands. The older woman looked up. "Oh! Maddie." She adjusted her glasses. "Thank you so much for all your help at the Mud Run. It was a tremendous success."

I shifted guiltily. "I thought so too." I hadn't skipped out on any assigned Mud Run tasks. But if I'd had true San Benedetto spirit, I wouldn't have left early.

"What can I do for you today?" Harriet smoothed the front of her pale yellow blouse.

"I'm still researching that goblet," I said. "Could I take a look at the materials Chadwick was working with?"

The corners of her mouth pulled downward. "I don't suppose it would hurt. Poor Chadwick. Poor Rea." She led me to a small library and settled me in at a square table with several boxes of files. "It's a lot," she warned.

I studied the boxes. They didn't look too bad. "No problem."

"Hm." She left the room, leaving the door open behind her.

I opened the first box. Chadwick had made photocopies of the articles he'd found interesting. This made things simpler for me. I wouldn't have to dig through collections he'd looked at and try to guess what mattered.

But there were a *lot* of papers. Forcing myself to ignore the sunshine beckoning through the paned window, I got to work.

An hour later, I paused at an article from the *Placer Times and Transcript*. It was dated September 18, 1851.

We regret to announce the death of Mr. Salvador Morales of San Joaquin County. He died due to a fall from his horse while inspecting his rancho. His wife reported him missing when the horse returned unattended. A search party found Mr. Morales's body, his head mangled in such a shocking manner as to cause almost instant death. His wife lost her senses upon learning the news, repeating that her husband's luck would die with him.

Her husband's luck would die with him? That was kind of a weird thing to say. I crossed my ankles beneath the chair. But the widow had been distraught.

My mouth puckered. Vincenzo had bought his property from her. Was she in her right mind when she'd sold the rancho? Was that why he'd gotten such a good price?

I shook my head. It didn't matter. She'd sold it. Right mind or not, it was old news and had nothing to do with Vincenzo's goblet.

Beneath that page was a photocopy of an old letter, written in Spanish. Chadwick had helpfully provided a typed translation beneath.

Dear Sister Maria—

Most truly you have all our sympathy in this bereavement, which it has pleased our Heavenly Father should come upon you and your dear Children. Little did I expect when I received your letter that it would contain such distressing intelligence. For he who is gone, we cannot grieve, as we are assured his sorrow and pains are at an end.

I had been very uncomfortable the last few weeks, because I had never answered your letters written to me in the spring. I had all the while intended writing, as the fears you confessed preyed upon my mind. But in consequence of my illness, I was by no means strong enough to bear it. I could not tell what I ought to write & what to leave unwritten. I have often wished to be there so that I might have the opportunity of judging for myself how matters stood, though I did not think it possible they could have turned out quite so bad.

Return to Catalonia and leave that wicked place behind. You and your children will always receive a heartfelt welcome in my home.

—Francesco

I dug through the box, forcing myself to take care with papers. But of course the letters from Maria to Francesco weren't in it. They'd gone on to Catalonia.

Thoughtful, I returned the letter to the box and kept plowing through the files. But I didn't find any mention of the goblet.

I made photocopies of the letter and stopped at Harriet's office. "I'm done. I put everything back in the box."

She looked up from behind her antique desk. "Thank you, Maddie. Did you find what you were looking for?"

"I'm not sure. I made photocopies of a few documents that looked promising though." I handed them to her across the desk.

Frowning, she adjusted her glasses and studied the pages. "These documents aren't ours."

I brushed back my hair. "But they were in the box."

"I'm sure they were. But we don't keep copies of articles from *The Placer Times and Transcript* here. That paper wasn't based in San Benedetto. And you say the letter and its transcription were in the box as well?"

"Yes..." I took the translation from her and studied it. Why would Chadwick have used a typewriter for the translation? No one used typewriters anymore.

My jaw hardened. Chadwick mustn't have translated the document. Someone else had.

A yellowed paper with handwriting on it had gone missing from Clayton's files. Other pages may have gone missing too. Had one of the letters I'd found at the Historical Association come from the warehouse?

"I take it this doesn't belong to you either?" I asked, pointing to the letter I'd copied.

She shrugged and returned the other photocopies to me. "It could. I'm not familiar with every scrap of paper in the association, but it doesn't look familiar."

"Well," I said, "thanks."

I returned to the museum. But instead of returning to work, I kept re-reading the letter.

The museum's wall phone rang. Absently, I answered. "San Benedetto Paranormal Museum. This is Maddie speaking."

"My son is on his way to Auburn," a voice like a crackling leaf said.

"Ah, Mrs. Linden?"

"Here is the address." She rattled off a string of numbers and hung up.

I wrote it down before I forgot it. If she was calling me about Herb's whereabouts, he must have the goblet with him. And he must have done something to really annoy her for her to rat him out. *Lucky Herb.*

I tore the page off my notepad and hurried out the door, the bell jangling above my head.

chapter twenty-three

ON THE BRICK SIDEWALK, I locked the museum's front door, giving it an extra tug to make sure it was locked. A gust of late morning fog chilled my skin. I zipped my museum hoodie higher.

The door to Mason's motorcycle shop snicked open. Detective Laurel Hammer strode outside, and I froze. Maybe if I stood really, really still, she wouldn't notice me. Because I did not need to deal with her right now.

Mason followed on her bootheels. "Hold on. That's not the point."

"Oh?" She turned and folded her arms over her sleek navy pantsuit. "Then what is the point?"

"This is garbage." He rattled a sheet of paper at her. "Why is she lying? Something is seriously wrong."

Or maybe freezing like a possum *wasn't* a reasonable avoidance strategy. But if I returned inside the museum, Laurel would hear the door. I edged toward Adele's tearoom.

The keys slipped from my fingers and clattered to the sidewalk. Hastily, I bent to retrieve them. I straightened, and Laurel scowled at me. Because of *course* she'd heard.

"Speak of the devil." A muscle throbbed in her jaw.

"Don't bring Maddie into this," Mason said sharply.

Her lip curled. "Isn't she already in it?"

"Ah… I'm just on my way to find Herb." I jerked my thumb toward my red pickup, parked beside a slender plum tree. "Museum business." *And not interfering in your investigation.*

"I knew you were cheating on him," Laurel hissed. "I *knew* it."

"What? Cheating on... whom?" But there was only one person I *could* be cheating on. *Jason.* My face flamed. "What are you talking about?"

"Belle left a letter on the fridge," Mason said. "I didn't notice it until today. It was folded, and kind of hidden, and..." He glowered at the detective. "I made the mistake of reporting it."

"What did it say?" I asked.

Mason's face reddened.

"That she left him because of his relationship with you," Laurel said.

"We don't have a relationship," Mason said. "Belle's wrong."

For no reason, an ache stabbed my chest. I took a step backward. Mason and I *did* have a relationship. We were friends.

"Sure." Laurel sneered. "That's why you ran straight to Maddie when your fiancée disappeared. That's why you two have been harassing suspects all over northern California."

"We're harassing—we're looking for Belle because Mason and I are friends," I said hotly. And why was I defending myself to Laurel?

Oh. Right. Because she was a cop, and this was an investigation. Though if Belle had really left because of a domestic dispute...

Ridiculous. I shook myself. I didn't believe that for a second.

"Grow up," she snapped. "Men and women can't be *just friends.*"

"I'm telling you," Mason said, "Maddie's innocent in this."

"But you're not?" Laurel arched a blond brow.

"Are you going to keep looking for Belle or not?" Mason growled.

Laurel snatched the paper from his hand. "We'll keep you posted." She strode to her blue muscle car, got inside, and roared off.

Mason shook his head. "Sorry, Mad. I had to... Sorry." He turned and walked into his shop.

A knot tightened my chest. But I knew better than to go after him. I turned and jerked back just in time to avoid slamming into Eliza.

Even though she was shorter than me, she managed to look down her hatchet nose. Her mouth scrunched with distaste. "So."

Terrific. Now Laurel's accusation would be all over Ladies Aid. And then my mother would be calling. "So nothing. Belle was wrong."

"Hmph." She adjusted the handbag over her arm, smoothed the pearl buttons on her tweed jacket. "I'm here to inform you that Ladies Aid has negotiated a deal with the owner of the furniture store. However, you'll have to act now."

"Deal?" I asked blankly.

"For the purchase."

I jammed my hands in my hoodie's pockets. "I don't have the money to buy that place."

"That can be worked out. We've been negotiating with the owner, and she's willing to compromise." Eliza named a price.

I gaped. That number was actually... reasonable. In fact, it was more than reasonable. "How?" I asked. Had Ladies Aid turned their hands to blackmail?

"It's a public good," she said. "It's for the town. The owner can deduct the loss on her taxes. But she can't wait."

"It's an amazing price," I said. *Suspiciously amazing.* "But I still don't have that kind of money."

"Of course you don't. Martha Manning's son is the president of the bank. We've arranged for a loan based upon a strict plan for acquiring donations. You will follow that plan to the letter. It's an astounding deal, and it took quite a bit of work by several of us to make it happen."

My insides roiled. "But I don't... I can't. This is too fast. I don't even have that 501c3 yet."

"We've got all the paperwork prepared for your nonprofit. All you need to do is sign. Now, come with me." She turned on her heel.

My heart beat loudly against my ribs. My feet rooted to the brick sidewalk.

She swiveled to face me. "Well? Are you going to start this new museum or not?"

"I— I mean— I have to find Herb." I hurried toward my vintage pickup.

"Didn't you hear what I said?" she called after me. "You have to act now. Today. The owner of the furniture store has another buyer. I had a hard time believing it, since it's sat vacant for so long. But I know the realtor's mother and she assures me it's true. She's only giving you a discount because of Ladies Aid. But this is a limited time offer."

"Then it's going to have to expire," I snapped. Climbing into my truck, I drove off, leaving Eliza gaping on the sidewalk.

My hands clenched on the over-sized wheel. It *had* been a good deal. A great deal. A once-in-a-lifetime deal. But I couldn't just jump into it. There were things to think about, like mission statements and...

I sagged against the worn seat. Who was I kidding? I wasn't a mission statement sort of person any more than I was a strict-donation-plan sort of person.

And so I'd panicked. Instead of listening thoughtfully and figuring things out, I'd panicked and run.

My pulse beat in my throat, my hands slackening on the wheel as I pulled onto the highway. I called myself a curator. But I ran a roadside attraction, not a museum.

I'd always been small-time, even when I'd worked overseas. I'd always been on the periphery of big things, my nose to the grindstone, doing the work for the sake of the work. I wasn't the kind of person who did big things.

I did small things, and oh God, was Jason going to see Belle's letter? Of course he would. Laurel would jam it in his face.

I almost called to tell him of course I wasn't cheating on him. But I was driving, and... It seemed weird to preemptively deny I'd been cheating.

He *had* to know there was nothing between Mason and me. Of *course* men and women could be just friends and neighbors.

Trees flashed past, then cars as I merged onto the freeway. I maneuvered around big rigs and tried to focus on the road instead of everything that was wrong with my life.

My phone rang on the passenger seat as I ascended the Sierra foothills, rising above the fog. I didn't answer, because I was driving. Also, I didn't want to talk to my mother.

I turned off the freeway and drove through a residential neighborhood, then into a more rural area. A sign for a Spanish-style winery flashed past. Oaks dotted the rolling hills, thick with tall, green grass.

I rolled down my window. The air here was cooler and dryer than I'd left behind in San Benedetto.

At a postbox marked *Morales*, I turned. The address Herb's mother had given me was at the end of the long driveway at the top of a lush, green hill. Horses grazed in a nearby corral.

I did not see Herb's yellow VW, and my stomach sank. Had I missed him again?

Steeling myself for disappointment, I walked up the neat cement steps to the front door. I rang the bell. It chimed inside the house.

After a minute or two, a young boy, his face covered in freckles opened the door. "Yeah?"

"Hi. I'm Maddie. Are your parents home?"

He turned his head. "Mom," he hollered.

Footsteps tread lightly down the tiled hallway. "Who is it?" a woman asked, appearing in the doorway. She wore jeans and a neat, button up blouse. "Yes?" The woman, presumably his mother, raked a hand through her mid-length brown hair. She was about my height and build, but she wore a few extra lines at the corners of her eyes.

"I'm sorry to bother you," I said. "I'm from the San Benedetto Paranormal Museum. I was looking for Herb Linden and thought he might be here. We work together."

"Oh, you just missed him."

I bit back a ripe word. *Herb.* "I don't suppose he asked you to de-curse a goblet for him?"

Her forehead puckered. "De-curse?"

Then she wasn't a shaman or mystic. My face warmed. "Sorry, there's been a mix-up. I thought he brought an old goblet to you." I took a step backward on the cement stoop, making to leave.

"No," she said, "he was here doing genealogical research."

I paused. "Genealogical?"

A calico cat paced around the corner of the hall and twined around the boy's ankles. He scooped up the cat and hugged her to his chest. The cat wriggled but didn't appear to take offense.

"We're descended from one of the Alta California rancheros," his mother continued. "Salvador Morales. Herb wanted a copy of our family tree. My aunt had once hired a genealogist, so we had a good bit of information." She ruffled her son's reddish hair. "Lucky for your friend, we'd just been working on our family tree for a school project."

"Yeah," I said. "Lucky. And you're really descendants of Salvador Morales?"

"Poor man. The story of his life has given us all sorts of material on California history. But my son's at an age where all that interests him is Salvador's gruesome death. I'm trying to spin that into the hazards of pioneer life, but..." She shrugged.

"His head was bashed in," her son said.

"Yeah," I said. "I heard that too."

"Boys," his mother said cheerfully. "They're all ghouls. I don't think they ever grow out of it."

"Did Herb say anything else to you?" I asked.

"Not really," she said. "Why? Is there a problem?"

"No, no. No problem. Thanks for your time." I made my way back to my pickup.

Genealogical research? I climbed into the truck and shut the door. Salvador Morales didn't have anything to do with the goblet. But Herb wouldn't be wasting his time on it, unless Salvador did...

Why did Herb care? And if I wasn't taking the collection, why did I?

chapter twenty-four

"MADELYN, THIS IS YOUR mother."

Phone to my ear, I bent my head and sighed. "I know." I propped my elbow on the ledge of the pickup's open window. I'd been avoiding this conversation all the way to Auburn. But I couldn't put it off any longer.

"Where are you?" she asked.

I looked around the Morales's front yard. In his corral, the horse flicked his tail. "Auburn," I said.

"What on earth are you doing way up there? You need to sign the papers here in San Benedetto."

I leaned my head against the rest and studied the pickup's roof. "I'm not signing the papers. I know you did a lot of work on this, but I didn't ask you to, and—"

"You're panicking," she said. The horse trotted to the metal fence.

I scowled, straightening. "Of course I'm panicking," I said. "This is happening way too fast."

"This building is a tremendous opportunity."

"Is it? I don't know. I don't know about any of this, because I still don't know what I'm doing with the collection."

"Like you knew what you were doing when you took over the paranormal museum?" she asked. "Or every time you started a job in a new country?"

"That was different."

"How?"

"I chose those countries. I didn't choose that furniture store." I'd also had a team in every country to support me, and I'd supported them in turn. Until they'd hung me out to dry.

"Madelyn—"

"Look, I'm sorry I'm not as successful as Melanie or Shane, but—"

She sucked in a breath. "That is not fair. I've never compared you to your brother and sister."

I rolled my eyes. *Sure.* "I need to figure this out for myself. And I don't like that furniture store."

"Why not?"

"It's mid-century monstrous, and the new collection isn't. That building doesn't fit."

The horse snorted. He trotted to a small red barn.

There was a long silence. "I see," my mother said finally. "And the 501c3 documents?"

"Can wait."

"You do realize that not making a decision is, in fact, making a decision? Doing nothing *is* a decision."

"I'm not doing nothing," I said, bumping the wheel with one knee. "I'm trying to figure out that goblet."

"Figure it out? What's to figure out?"

"I'm not sure. Just... there's something weird about its story. Look, I'll talk to you later. Bye." I hung up. Then for good measure, I turned off my phone.

I was right, and she knew it. These were big decisions. They couldn't be rushed into. I didn't even have a mission statement yet. How could I sign legal documents or take out a bank loan without a mission statement?

But as I drove down the mountain to San Benedetto, my gut churned. Was I making the right non-decision?

No, I knew what I was doing. My museum—such as it was—was a success. I'd come up with new ways to market it, and my ideas had worked. I was doing well. I could trust my instincts, and my instincts said that furniture store wasn't right.

Yeah.

Without quite realizing it, I found myself cruising through the adobe arch and onto San Benedetto's Main Street toward the museum. My stomach grumbled, and I glanced at the dash clock. It was past one.

I smiled. So I wasn't on autopilot to the museum after all. My stomach had been guiding me toward the taqueria.

I cruised past the museum. Clusters of women stood on the sidewalk outside the Fox and Fennel, Adele's tearoom. It was a Monday—not a big day for any of the downtown businesses. Frowning, I pulled into a nearby spot and walked back.

"Hey," I said to one of the women. "What's going on?"

"Oh." She brushed back a lock of graying hair. "We're just waiting for a table. You'll have to get in line, I'm afraid."

"Thanks." Thoughtful, I walked to the taqueria and bought a veggie burrito. Instead of eating it there, I returned to the museum.

GD, lying atop the old-fashioned cash register, flicked his ear when I walked inside. The bell jangled overhead.

I unwrapped my burrito on the counter and sat. A gap beneath the molding on the opposite wall marked the spot where the photo of Cora Gale and her husband had hung before water had ruined it. My chest hollowed at the sight. I'd need to do something about that empty space.

The bookcase door swiveled open. Adele walked into the museum, her high heels clicking on the checkerboard floor. "I thought I saw you walk past."

I shoved a grease-spotted bag of tortilla chips toward her. "Want one?"

"No, thanks. Is it true you're moving the museum into that furniture store?"

Did I imagine the eagerness in her tone? I hunched on the high stool. "No."

"Oh." Beneath her Jackie-Kennedy style pink suit, her shoulders dropped a fraction.

I studied her. "Adele, be honest. Do you want to expand your tearoom?"

"I don't need to."

Need and *want* were two different animals. I set my burrito on top of the flattened paper bag and angled my head toward the window and the women lined up outside. "Really?"

She studied my front window. The fog had thickened. I knew all she could see was gray. "Things *are* getting busier," she admitted. "It's only because tourists get here too early for wine tasting and realize they have to do something."

"It's nearly two o'clock. The wine tasting started hours ago, and you're past the lunch rush."

"But it's Monday. Lots of the wineries are closed."

I raised an eyebrow. Adele was a terrible liar. It was one of her many excellent qualities.

"I'll figure something out," she said. "It's fine."

I looked down at the burrito. Beans and cheese seeped out onto the paper bag.

No, the situation wasn't fine. And neither was I. My mom was right, I was passing up an opportunity, and out of what? Fear? My excuses had been mostly cope. I could figure out how to turn the museum into a successful nonprofit.

And I wasn't on my own. I had a team of helpers here too. My friends had been *trying* to help me. Just, maybe not the right way. Maybe it *was* time for a new challenge. But on my terms.

I drew a tortilla chip from the white paper bag. "Well, that's too bad then. Because I am moving the museum."

Her eyes widened. "You are? Where?"

"Don't know. I'm going to get right on that after I finish this burrito."

On the register, the black cat sneezed.

"It won't be easy," Adele warned.

"Finding a new location can't be as hard as moving GD into it," I joked, then sobered.

GD's tail lashed.

How *was* I going to move the cat? The last time I'd tried to transport him anywhere, one of us had regretted it. And it hadn't been GD.

I shook my head. I'd figure that out too.

The realtor smiled brightly. She was a tall, elegant blond of a certain age. And I'd learned the hard way that she was determined.

She motioned to the overhead industrial lights. "Imagine the charm!"

I had a supernaturally vivid imagination. But not even I could conjure charm out of this corrugated metal building.

A ghostly draft whispered across my skin. Divots had fallen from the walls, sunlight making pin spots on the cement floor. Something rustled beneath the crumpled newspapers lying in one dusty corner.

"The size is right," I said, trying to inject cheer into my voice. It echoed in the vast warehouse. "But we're a bit far from town."

It was the fifth location we'd scouted, each one moving farther and farther from the town center. I told myself I was lucky the realtor had had time today at all. I'd only made the appointment yesterday after my chat with Adele.

The realtor grimaced. "All right. There's one more place on my list that might work."

"Sixth time's a charm," I said brightly.

"Right," she said with less enthusiasm.

I got into her Audi. The realtor aimed it back toward town, so that was a relief.

"It's near a new mixed-use development," she said. "And only three blocks from a vineyard. You did say your museum attracts wine tourists?"

I nodded. Three blocks from a vineyard wouldn't be bad. Though I was getting sick of all the lookalike mixed-use developments. And I wondered how their residents would feel about living next to a paranormal tourist attraction.

Ten minutes later, we pulled in front of a three-story faux-stone building with shops on the bottom and apartments on top. A vineyard spilled across the land on its left.

"Here we are," she said, stepping from the car.

I exited and came to stand beside her. "Where is it?" There was no way my museum was going into one of those mixed-use places. The neighbors would hate it, and that fake stone looked more corporate than fairytale.

"Right there." She pointed to a flat stretch of land covered in weeds. "Have you ever considered building your own museum?"

"The land? You're talking about the land?" Land wasn't on my real estate wish list. I didn't know *how* to build a museum to spec.

"Imagine. You can create exactly what you want for your museum. You could even build secret passages."

I never should have put *secret passage* on that wish list. "Ah..."

"Just think. Your dream museum could be right *here*."

I swallowed. *Was* this the answer? Build my own museum? Maybe I didn't have to know how to do it. After all, that's what architects were for. *And architects cost money.* "How much?"

She named a figure, and I swallowed. *Good Lord.* It wasn't as bad as land in some parts of California, but it was a lot. I might be able to raise the funds though.

"Building my own's not a bad idea," I said, grudging. "But it's a new idea to me. I'll have to think about it."

A woman emerged from the faux-stone building. I squinted. *Belle?*

"Ah, could you wait a moment?" I asked.

Not waiting for an answer, I hurried toward the woman. It *was* Belle. Her hair was black, but it was definitely Belle.

chapter twenty-five

AND THEN I DID something stupid.

"Belle?" I shouted.

The woman turned toward me. Belle's eyes widened. She raced to an aging red Porsche, parked on the street beside the faux-stone building.

"Wait," I yelled, jogging after her. "I want to help you."

She hopped inside the sports car and revved the engine.

I reached its bumper. The car zipped from its parking spot and roared down the street.

Cursing, I ran back to the realtor's gray Audi. "We have to follow her."

Ambling toward her car, the realtor brushed a length of blond hair over one shoulder. "What? Why?"

"She's thinking of listing her property," I lied. "It might be right for my museum. I should have thought of it before."

She sauntered to the driver's side. "Are you sure she wants to sell? Because it looked like she was running from you."

The Porsche made a left turn and vanished from view behind a construction site.

"She thought I was someone else." I got into the car and shut the door.

She settled herself inside, checked her perfect makeup in the mirror, took a sip of her latte. Starting the car, she turned to me and smiled. "Let's see what your friend has to say about that property."

"I wouldn't exactly say friend—"

The Audi screeched from its spot, rocking my head against the rest. A horn blared behind us.

"Holy sh—" The rest of the word was lost as we whipped around the corner so fast gravity plastered me to the door. The realtor might have started slow, but she was a flyer. At least when a commission was at stake.

We rocketed down a straight road, vineyards blurring outside my window.

No one was in front of us though. Belle must have turned off the road somewhere. By now she probably thought she'd lost us, which she had. And right now I was okay with that. I thought it might be nice to live to see forty.

"Do you see her?" the realtor asked.

My knuckles whitened on the door handle. "Gagh—"

"Oh, *there* she is." She accelerated, and we flew around another corner, tires screaming.

I cleared my throat. "You know. Her property might not be *quite* right for the museum."

"Do you know if she has a listing agent yet?"

"Ah... I don't... Uh..."

"It's all right. I can look it up." One handed, she reached behind her and dug her phone from her purse, kept in a net holder between the seats. The Audi swerved into the oncoming lane.

A farm truck loaded with onions trundled toward us.

"Let's look it up later," I said, voice thin.

"No, no. I can do it." The realtor spun the wheel, and we arced around another corner. The onion truck's horn blatted. Belle's Porsche appeared a quarter mile in front of us. The realtor studied her phone. "What's the address?"

I gulped. "I can't remember."

"Just give me the street," she said, eyes glued to the screen. "I'll find it."

"No, no," I said wildly. "I really can't remember. You can stop—Oh my God!"

A raccoon waddled across the road. It looked over its shoulder at us. Its brown eyes widened.

She yanked the wheel, and we careened around the animal. "I hate trash pandas. Filthy animals."

"Yeah." My chuckle had a maniacal edge, but she didn't seem to notice. I checked the rearview mirror. The raccoon stood on its hind legs and swayed, one paw pressed to its heart. "Wouldn't want one of those on your bumper."

"No, indeed." She shuddered. We closed on the Porsche.

"Ah, maybe ease up a little?" I said. "We don't want her to think we're chasing her down."

She laughed merrily. "No, we wouldn't want to spook her. Would we?" Obligingly, she released the gas, and the Audi slowed. She dropped her phone into an empty cupholder. "So tell me more about this property."

My breathing steadied. "It's a, ah, commercial property. Fifteen thousand square feet. Ish. It's got a big parking lot." I *would* need a decent-sized parking lot.

"How many stories?"

"One," I said. "Well, the entrance is a raised section, but it's mostly one big open space."

That would make my imaginary building easier to remodel. Throwing up walls was easy. Cramped rooms to wander through would be more atmospheric than a wide-open, gallery-type space. And having to descend to the museum proper would add more psychological bang.

"Oh," she said. "That means stairs. Is it ADA compliant for people who can't manage them?"

"There's a wheelchair elevator." I eyed the Porsche. It seemed to be slowing.

"And you're willing to do some remodeling?"

"Within reason," I said. "I'm not sure how much of a budget I'll have for upgrades, so I want to be conservative."

The Porsche turned down a dirt road. Dust plumes rose behind its tires.

"What you're describing sounds so familiar," she mused. "I'm sure I've seen her property."

Since it didn't exist, that was unlikely. My fingernails dug into the door handle.

"Now where was it?" the realtor continued, turning after Belle's car.

We passed a field covered in yellow wildflowers. The Porsche turned again, heading toward a ramshackle barn.

"Not *here*, I think," she said.

We pulled into a junkyard. A *Beware of Dog* sign hung at a lopsided angle from its low, barbed wire fence. Cars in varying stages of decay lay scattered outside the gray barn. Belle walked inside it.

"Ah..." I swiveled to face her. "I have a confession to make."

Her forehead puckered. "She doesn't have a property for sale, does she?"

My realtor might have the driving skills of a demon from a teen slasher flick, but she was no dummy. "No," I admitted. "I just really needed to follow her. She's wanted for questioning in connection to a murder, and—"

"Murder?" she yelped. "Why didn't you say so?" She snatched her phone from the cupholder. "I'll call the cops."

I should have thought to do that. After all, I was dating one. "Ask for Laurel Hammer or Jason Slate. They're the detectives on the case." I opened the door and stepped from the Audi.

"Where are you going?" she asked.

"To see what's going on."

"I'll keep the car running. Just in case."

"Thanks." Considering the massive lies I'd just admitted to, she was being awfully cool about all this. I walked toward the barn.

Free tickets to my museum didn't seem like adequate compensation for the afternoon's wild ride. Flowers? A cake? I edged to the side of the open barn door.

Yes, definitely a cake. Maybe a bundt. I liked bundts. Especially lemon poppyseed. I scanned the yard for a dog. The warning sign was probably a bluff.

"...don't care what kind of car," Belle was saying. "As long as it drives and isn't too flashy."

A man's voice responded, but I couldn't catch the words. I leaned in and looked around. The inside of the barn was even more jumbled than the exterior. Wherever Belle and her friend were, they were hidden. Which hopefully meant they couldn't see me either.

"Don't worry about that," she said. "I'll have the money tomorrow."

The man's voice rose on a question.

She laughed. "You think *she's* not good for it? She'll pay."

There was a clank. Belle's voice grew quieter, as if she were moving further away. I gnawed my bottom lip.

A low growl sounded off to my right. All the hair stood at attention on the back of my neck. Slowly, I turned.

A massive black pit bull with two thick streams of drool cascading from its fangs watched me. Its bronze-colored eyes narrowed.

Skin clammy, I backed from the barn. I have an unhealthy respect for angry dogs. I like dogs just fine. But where I'd worked overseas, aggressive dogs had been left to run wild. Even dogs with owners had often been treated so badly they bit passersby for the fun of it.

The dog paced toward me. He lowered his head.

"Hey." I smiled, heart thumping. "Hi, pooch."

The pit bull lunged.

I pivoted and hightailed it back to the car. The realtor—bless her—leaned across the seat and swung the passenger door open.

I dove inside and slammed the door shut behind me. The pit bull leapt, pawing at the window and barking.

"Drive, drive, drive," I shouted.

She backed from the lot at speed, swinging the car around fast enough to spin our own dust devil. We bulleted down the dirt road, the dog in hot pursuit.

A blue muscle car whipped past in the opposite direction. *Laurel.*

I considered warning her about the pit bull. But since she wasn't in the habit of taking my calls and the dog was right there in the road...

I settled back in my seat. She'd figure it out.

chapter twenty-six

"What I don't understand," Jason said, "is why you didn't call me from the car."

I gave the glass display case another swipe with my dust cloth. Visitors wandered through the museum. A woman stopped to take a picture of GD, staring hard at a dust mote.

What I didn't understand was why Jason hadn't said anything about Belle's letter. I hoped it was because he trusted me, and if so, I was grateful. But I was still surprised he hadn't brought it up.

"I was busy keeping the car from crashing," I said.

"But you weren't driving." Jason folded his arms, rumpling the fabric of his navy suit.

I lifted the lid on the case and spritzed the inside of the glass with cleaner. "I was keeping us from crashing through the sheer power of my will. Trust me, it worked. I'm here, aren't I?"

His gaze flicked toward the white ceiling. "Tell me again what you heard at the junk yard."

Belle had managed to evade Laurel. And Jason wasn't giving me any details on how that had happened. This meant Laurel was embarrassed and furious. And *that* meant I would be even deeper on her bad side than usual.

My hand clenched on the cleaning bottle. "Belle said she needed a new car," I said. "She was getting money tomorrow, and she was getting it from a woman."

"But you don't have any idea who."

I plucked a white ceramic hand from the case and buffed it. "No. She implied the woman wouldn't have any trouble paying. But since we don't know how much money we're talking about, that doesn't help narrow things down. Unless you *do* know how much money we're talking about?"

He shook his head. "We brought in the guy at the junkyard. He wasn't forthcoming and lawyered up."

"Well, damn. That's not surprising at all." I returned the plaster hand to its case.

The wall phone rang behind the counter, and I winced. Leo plucked the receiver from the wall and answered.

"Problems?" Jason asked.

"Mrs. Grandall. She's called three times so far today about that stupid goblet. The woman's obsessed."

"I understand she takes her family history very seriously," he said, bland. "Now let's go over this again."

I sighed. "Honestly, I've told you everything I heard."

"Then let's go back to the other suspects you've talked to."

I shifted the white hand on top of a spirit board inside the display case. "I haven't seen Dr. Milford MacDuff since we last talked."

"Do we have any reason to believe Chadwick was going to spill the beans about writing his dissertation for him?"

"No," I said, reluctant. "But maybe Chadwick was blackmailing him. He seemed to have a very long rope when it came to working at the ACHA and pursuing his own interests."

"And he killed Rea because she knew about the blackmail?"

I nodded. "Presumably."

Jason grunted. "Is that all? I figured you'd have more by now."

I smiled, warmth spreading through my chest. I loved that we could talk these things over without pesky accusations of interfering in his investigation. "Hey, that's quality intel."

"And I do appreciate it." He ran his hand down my arm.

"And then there's Bob."

"And then there's Bob," he agreed. "I hate to say it, but my instincts tell me he didn't kill his wife. He loved her. And yes, I know I can be fooled. I'm just saying it doesn't feel right."

"Whoa. You're following your instincts and not just the evidence? What happened to you?"

He grinned. "All this time spent in your museum has rubbed off on me. Who else?"

I moved another hand, this one with a neat men's cuff, beside the other two. "Chadwick's brother, Price, has been suspiciously helpful."

Jason shook his head. "It's not good enough."

"I know. All our suspects are oddly unsatisfying." I studied the polished white hands. "I feel like I'm missing something." *But what?*

"Me too." He clawed a hand over his dark, curling hair. "Laurel and I have been going around and around on it and are getting nowhere. Belle's connected to this though. I can't think of another reason why she'd run."

"Is she an actual suspect?"

"A person of interest. She and Chadwick knew each other, but we can't find a motive. All we know is he died, and she ran. It's not looking good for her."

My stomach made an uneasy barrel roll. *Poor Mason. Poor Jordan.* I wondered if Jordan knew the truth yet, or if Mason had managed to keep up the business-trip fiction.

"You okay?" Jason asked.

"Yeah. I just get the feeling that this isn't going to have a happy ending."

He grimaced. "You can't fix everything. That's something I've learned in this job the hard way."

"I know," I said quietly. But that knowledge didn't make me feel any better.

"Have you come to any conclusions about the museum?"

"I have concluded that I will not do me, the museum, or Clayton's collection any favors by rushing into things. There are a lot of pieces that need to fit together, and that's going to take some planning. And not by Ladies Aid. By me. It's my collection. Or it will be."

"You're right to take it slow."

"I am?"

He kissed me. "It's worked for us."

I rested my head against his chest and loosely looped my arms around his waist. He felt so good. We felt good together. He trusted me, and I was lucky to have his steady presence in my life.

Since we were in the museum and neither of us were big on PDAs, we settled for murmured goodbyes, and he left. I finished cleaning the case and returned to the counter.

"Mrs. Grandall called," Leo said.

Augh. I massaged my temples. *Her again?* "Let me guess. She wanted an update on the goblet."

"Yeah." He rubbed the back of his neck. "Mrs. Grandall sounded kind of... annoyed. She said... Uh... Hold on." He pulled a scrap of paper from the pocket of his leather jacket. "If she can't count on you to manage one simple item, you won't be able to count on her support for the new museum."

My mouth firmed. Since I hadn't counted on her support from the get-go, that wasn't much of a disappointment. Though she did seem to know a lot about museum management.

But this business with Herb had gone on long enough. I called my paranormal collector.

To my surprise, he answered. "Yes?" he asked cautiously.

"The goblet. What's the story?"

"It's not—"

"I don't care if it's not properly bound. I just want to know what's going on. You owe me that."

Herb huffed a breath. "The Wok and Bowl. Thirty minutes." He disconnected.

"Well?" Leo raised a brow.

"We're rendezvousing at the Wok and Bowl."

"Cool. Pick me up some Mongolian beef, will you?"

"Mission accepted." I zipped up my paranormal museum hoodie and walked to my pickup, parked in the brick alley. As I pulled down the narrow street, I couldn't help glancing up at Mason's apartment windows. A curtain shifted.

My hands tightened, the keys digging into my raw palms. Was it Jordan? Mason?

Belle?

I shook my head. *Not my problem.* Not right now, at least. I drove to the Wok and Bowl and claimed a linoleum table overlooking the bowlers.

Pins clattered. The scent of Chinese food wafted through the air. Waitresses in poodle skirts swished past carrying trays of food.

My breathing slowed as I remembered all the times I'd bowled here as a teen and eaten here as an adult. I was going to miss this place.

And though I knew San Benedetto couldn't—shouldn't—stay frozen in time, nostalgia gripped my heart. Why did so many old and lovely things have to go away?

Herb slid into the chair opposite me and looked around. "Did you come alone?" He straightened his bowtie.

I angled my head. "Really?" His suspicion had gotten old long ago. Did he really think I'd brought the fuzz?

"Did you?" he asked, his voice rising.

Just play along. "Yes," I said in a strained voice. "I came alone. Why? Is someone after you?" I pushed the cup of coffee I'd ordered for him across the table.

He grabbed the white mug and took a sip. "You do hang around with that cop a lot."

Because *that cop* was my boyfriend, which Herb well knew. I sighed. "All right." I laced my hands together on the table. "Tell me about the curse on the goblet."

"A long time ago, when I was a child, I caught wind of a story. I can't tell you where I heard it, or if I read it, because I don't remember. I just remember the story."

I raised a brow. "Which is?"

"That the Benedetto goblet wasn't always the Benedetto goblet. It belonged to someone else before Vincenzo."

"To whom? Salvador Morales?"

He blinked. "You knew?"

Ha! A warm, satisfied, petty glow spread through my rotten soul. I liked having surprised Herb. "I talked to the Morales family after you left their house," I said, smug.

He straightened in his chair. "My own *mother* narced on me?" Bowling pins rattled.

"The unkindest cut of all. Now, the only reason I could figure you'd ask them about their family history was if it was in relation to the goblet. And the goblet came from Spain, and Salvador was from Spain—"

"Catalonia."

"Right," I said. "That part of Spain. So... what? Did Vincenzo get the goblet when he bought the rancho?"

"Stole the rancho, you mean." Herb's lips pursed.

Right. Because what was a ghost story without drama? "I know he bought it for a song. And maybe that was less than ethical. But—"

"He forced that poor woman to sell after he murdered her husband." His thick spectacles flashed beneath the overhead lights.

I blinked. "Murdered? You have evidence of this?"

"Of course I don't. I told you, all I had was the story of the murder. The goblet was lucky for Salvador Morales. But it became a curse for his killer, Vincenzo. That's why the curse is so hard to remove. There's blood involved. But I've located another curse box. It's in Norway, and the cost of shipping's atrocious. But—"

I flattened my palm on the linoleum table. "Hold on. You're going on rumor? You have no actual evidence?"

"No, but Solomon did."

Oh, boy. "Clayton's father? Is that where you heard the rumor from?" I'd never met Solomon Clarke. But by all accounts he'd been even battier about the paranormal than Herb. His say-so wasn't exactly reliable.

"Are you kidding? That guy wouldn't give me the time of day if he was wearing three watches and standing beneath the town clock. I can't remember where I heard the rumor. But I did talk to him about it once. He told me it was true, but he wouldn't tell me how he knew." His mouth pinched. "Solomon could be a real jerk."

"I've heard that," I said evenly. Solomon had also had a reputation for trafficking in stolen goods. This was another reason to give this donated gift horse a good look in the mouth. "So what do you think of the rest of his collection?"

The little man's gaze turned misty. "It's the premier paranormal collection in North America. Don't get me wrong, there are amazing artifacts in the hands of others. But as a collection, as a whole? This is historic."

"You think I should keep it?"

Herb's eyes widened behind his thick lenses. "Was there ever any question?" His thin lips compressed. "I can't blame you for accepting it. I'd do the same thing. I know you won't need me anymore, that this is the end of our partnership. I *still* think Dion Fortune's scrying mirror would be an excellent addition for you, but..." He drew himself up. "I can be the better man about this. And maybe, if you need to sell anything off, you'll think of me?" He leaned closer, his eyebrows lifting.

"Absolutely." My heart twinged. As much as Herb drove me crazy, this *would* change our relationship. I'd be seeing less of him. And that made me... sad.

He pushed back his chair and stood. "It's been an honor working with you." He held out his hand, and I shook it.

"One more thing," I said. "Why did you run away with the goblet like that? Why all the secrecy?"

He winced. "At first I took it because it was dangerous. And I was kind of angry. But then... I just don't have all the answers about the goblet yet. And I didn't want you to think less of me. My ego got in the way. I'm sorry."

"I still think you're the best paranormal collector in California."

Herb sneered. "Only California? Try the west coast." He stalked from the bowling alley, and I smiled.

chapter twenty-seven

IT WAS ONLY AFTER Herb had left that I realized he hadn't agreed to return the goblet. Hopefully, that was one of those things that didn't have to be said; it was understood. Bowling pins clattered, and I flinched.

The red-headed waitress swished to the table, her poodle skirt swinging. She deposited a white paper bag in front of me. "Here you go."

"Thanks." I paid in cash and stood.

"Oh, Maddie." Mr. Chang, in neat khakis and a vintage red and white bowling shirt, strode toward my table and smiled. "Do you want to buy a bowling ball?"

"Is it haunted? Cursed? Lucky?"

He stopped short. "Uh, no. I just thought I'd give you a heads up in case you wanted anything."

My heart heavied. "It's really happening then?"

He nodded. "It looks like it. Nothing's been signed, but like I said, I have a very interested buyer."

I looked around the wide space and swallowed. "And they're definitely not keeping it as a bowling alley?"

"No. It's going to be knocked down. I pretty much expected that, but... I'll be sad to see the old girl go. We can't stop change though. I mean, look at you, expanding your museum."

"Yeah," I said, thoughtful. "You can't stop change. Excuse me, I need to, ah... go."

I hurried from the bowling alley and to my pickup. Was it possible? Had I been missing the obvious?

Instead of returning to the museum, I detoured to Ladies Aid. I climbed the concrete steps and knocked on the black door of the fifties-era building.

After a minute or so, a silver-haired woman I didn't know well peered out. She adjusted her glasses on her beaklike nose. "Madelyn Kosloski?"

"Yes, is Anne here?"

"I believe so. Come in." She held the door wider, and I walked into the foyer.

The old lady led me to the sitting room. Light from the high windows knifed across its rose-patterned wallpaper, bookshelves, and paintings.

I spotted Anne knitting in one of the high-backed chairs. "Thanks," I said to my escort and walked toward the retired history teacher. "Anne?"

The white-haired woman looked up. "Maddie? What a delightful surprise." She set her knitting in a cloth bag beside her chair. Straightening, she adjusted her fluffy pink cardigan. "What brings you back to Ladies Aid? Are you thinking of joining?"

I shuddered. "No." A *bazillion times no.* "I've been doing more digging into the Benedetto goblet."

"And have you learned anything interesting?"

"It's from Spain." I sat in the matching chair across from her. "Catalonia, to be specific."

Anne blinked guilelessly.

"Just like Salvador Morales," I finished.

Her lips pursed. "I suppose Vincenzo Benedetto could have acquired the goblet when he purchased Salvador's rancho."

"I also found the newspaper article about Salvador's death."

"A fall from a horse," she said promptly.

In the wingchair, I crossed my legs. "Yes, a fall. And I found a letter from Maria Morales's brother, Francesco."

Her eyes widened. "Really?"

"The letter implied that something bad was happening at the rancho. Francesco expressed regret he hadn't answered sooner, and shock that things had gone so wrong. The letter implied there was more going on than a one-time fall from a horse, fatal as it may have been."

"Fascinating," she murmured, drumming her fingers on the soft arm of the chair. "Do you have the letter?"

"I forgot to bring it with me. I'm sorry." And I really was. Anne would have enjoyed reading it. Silently, I vowed to make her a copy.

Anne leaned forward, her fog-colored eyes twinkling with interest. "Where on earth did you find it?"

"I didn't. Chadwick Keegan filched it from Solomon Clarke's warehouse office. The letter belonged to Solomon."

It was a guess, but an educated one. Chadwick had a laptop and modern printers to work with. Using a typewriter for the translation seemed like the sort of thing old Solomon Clarke would have done.

And Chadwick *had* taken papers from that collection. Why *wouldn't* they have ended up in his files at the San Benedetto Historical Association?

"That poor murdered boy." Anne tsked and shook her head.

My breath caught. *Chadwick? Or Salvador?* "Do you know anything about problems at the rancho before Salvador had his accident?"

"Well," Anne said, "there was the fire."

"Fire?"

"The barn burned down. He lost most of his horses, the poor beasts." She clucked her tongue. "Such a tragedy."

"And the fire happened...?"

Two elderly women in fluffy cardigans tottered into the sitting room. Speaking in low tones, they made for the samovar.

"About a month before Salvador's accident," Anne said. "There was a silly story that he'd died of a broken heart after the loss of his horses. So ridiculous. A broken heart doesn't make you fall from a horse." She cocked her white head, her brows lifting. "Though a heart attack might."

I leaned forward, bracing my forearms on my thighs. "And Vincenzo Benedetto? When did he move here?"

"You should know this," Anne said in a severe tone. "The town was founded in 1852, after Vincenzo bought the rancho and broke it up into parcels. Vincenzo arrived in March of 1851. He started a small and unsuccessful farm on the outskirts of Salvador's rancho. Vincenzo's land was terrible. Unlike the rancho, there was no water source on Vincenzo's farm."

"That must have caused some conflicts."

"Water rights in California have always caused conflicts," she said. "Vincenzo was lucky he was able to purchase that rancho, and for a song."

"Yes," I said absently. Could Herb have been right about foul play? "Lucky."

"Did you find anything else?" she asked.

I blinked, refocusing, and shifted in the high-backed chair. "No. Just the one letter and an article from the *Placer Times and Transcript* about Salvador's fall."

She tapped a gnarled finger to her chin. "You know... I may be able to access more articles from that paper concerning Salvador, if you like."

"Oh, you don't have to—"

"Nonsense." She waved off my objection. "I love a good spot of historical research."

I smiled. "I'm surprised you're not a member of the Historical Association."

"Politics." She shook her head. "I despise it, and it's in every organization, including the Historical Association."

Seriously? What was there to get political about in a local historical association? "And Ladies Aid?"

"That's different. Ladies Aid *matters.*" She smiled. "You'll understand when you become a member."

My insides chilled. "Heh, heh." I rose hastily. "Well, thank you. Anything you can find would be great." Not that I expected much. But you never knew.

I returned to the museum and handed Leo the paper bag with his food. "Here you go. Sorry, it might be a little cold." On the glass counter, GD sniffed the bag with professional interest.

My assistant pressed his hand to the bottom of the white bag. "Thanks. And it's still warm. I'm going to eat this in the Fortune Telling Room."

"I'll man the counter," I said.

GD growled. The black cat flicked his tail.

"Oh, stop it," I told him and scanned the main room. Three guests wandered its aisles. "It's my counter." Even if the cat thought it was his. I thought all sorts of things that eventually turned out to be wrong. It was time GD got used to being wrong too.

The bell over the front door jangled. Mason strode inside in his typical black jeans and tee.

I stiffened. "Oh, hi."

He ran his hand over his blond head. "I heard you found Belle and called the cops."

My stomach tightened. This was what I'd been afraid of. He'd think I'd betrayed her. Or worse, betrayed him and Jordan. But the police were already looking for Belle. What did he expect me to do? Not report it? "I had to—"

He raised his broad hand. "I know. Jason wouldn't give me the details. What happened?"

"I spotted Belle leaving that new mixed-use complex beside the vacant lot out by Santania Winery. You know the one?"

He nodded. "I know it. One of the women who works with Belle at the salon lives there. The cops went to talk to her. She said Belle spent the night. She said—" His face reddened.

My nostrils flared. I could guess the rest. Belle had probably said she was escaping Mason.

I cleared my throat. "Anyway, I followed her to that junkyard in the old barn off Merlot Avenue. It sounded like she was trying to make a deal for a new car. It also sounded like she was going to get money from someone. A woman."

He nodded. "Probably from her friend from the salon. Belle told her I was... violent."

My chest hardened. It was a heinous accusation. There were violent men in the world, and spousal abuse was still all too common. But Mason wasn't one of those men.

We'd been together before Belle had returned to his life. He was a good man, and an honorable one. And he'd never attack someone weaker than him—man or woman.

But no one wanted to believe Belle had been lying about Mason, because it was horrible. And it also cast unfair doubt on all the women who weren't lying about domestic abuse.

A vein pulsed at Mason's temple. "Someone from child protective services showed up at my place this morning," he said, voice level. "They talked to Jordan."

Protective...? I swayed, sickened, and pressed my hand on the cool counter. "Oh, no. Does he know his mother—?"

"No." He shook his head. "They didn't tell him Belle had taken off. But he's starting to ask questions. I'm not sure how to answer them anymore."

"And protective services... Did they... What's the next step?" If they took Jordan, it would break Mason.

"I don't know," he said, his voice low. "They wouldn't tell me anything. But Jordan's still in my home, and that's what counts." Unspoken were the words, *for now.*

chapter twenty-eight

THE BOOKCASE SWUNG OPEN. My paranormal collector peered through his thick glasses into the museum. I'd turned the sign in the window to CLOSED this fog-bound Thursday evening. But a few guests still wandered the aisles.

"Is the coast clear?" Herb whispered.

I made a show of looking around. No spies in trench coats and fedoras lurked between the aisles. "We haven't been compromised," I said gravely.

He sidled into the museum, and the bookcase shut silently behind him. A brown paper shopping bag dangled from his fingers.

Like liquid oil, GD slithered from the haunted rocking chair. The cat stalked toward him.

"Tell me that's the goblet," I said.

"Not so loud." Herb's gaze darted around the museum. GD sniffed at the bag in his hands.

I forced my hands to unclench. *Patience.*

He set the paper bag on the glass counter. Standing on tiptoes, I looked inside without touching it.

A wooden box with a glass lid on it lay within. The goblet was on a stand against red velvet backing. He might be irritating as a hot rash, but Herb had done a bang-up job with the presentation.

I lifted my brows. "Wow."

"The binding box wasn't cheap," he warned.

Of course it wasn't. Life was one bill after another, and being short on cash was the story of mine. But I shrugged half-heartedly. "How much?"

The little man named a figure. Briefly, I closed my eyes, tamping down my annoyance. Herb *knew* I was on a razor-thin budget.

When I'd mastered myself, I said, "There's only one problem."

"Is it the red velvet?" he asked anxiously. "I know it clashes with the blue straw inside. But the straw seemed to disappear against a blue velvet backing."

"No, it's the ownership. I'm not sure the goblet really belongs to me."

Herb's jaw hardened. "You can't still be thinking of turning down Clayton's donation? I thought you'd gotten over that. For heaven's sake, Maddie, put your cowgirl pants on."

"You're mixing your metaphors. I think you mean put on your big-girl pants. Or maybe cowgirl up."

"You know what I mean." His eyes sparked dangerously behind his coke-bottle glasses.

"I meant the Morales family."

"Oh." He smoothed his bow tie. "I suspect a legal claim to the goblet would be difficult to prove. It's not likely Vincenzo stole the goblet off Salvador's body. The most likely scenario is that he purchased it along with other effects from the rancho when his widow sold."

"And yet," I said, "there's a curse on the goblet. Those don't just happen. And you said it was a blood curse."

"I didn't think you believed in curses."

But I was starting to. That said, I didn't want to give up my reputation as a paranormal agnostic.

I gave him what I hoped was an enigmatic smile. "I think I'd like to talk to them about the goblet anyway. Whether they have a legal claim or not, it once belonged to their ancestor. They're a part of the story."

"We have no proof it first belonged to Salvador," Herb warned.

"Maybe the family will, though. Old letters, old documents... Even though Maria returned to Spain—"

"But she didn't. She took her family to San Francisco."

"That just increases the odds the Morales family would have some useful documents." I drummed my fingers on the counter.

I couldn't blame Maria for staying in California. Her brother had sounded like an ass. *Sorry I didn't write when you told me about all the problems you were having. Sooo busy...*

A far-off siren sounded, and Herb gave a start. "Gotta go."

"Herb—"

He beetled out the front door. The bell jingled in his wake. I stared down at the bag he'd left. At least he hadn't run off with the goblet again.

I set it on the shelf beneath the old-fashioned register and sold a few Tarot decks and books to departing guests. Soon GD and I were alone. Locking the front door, I turned to my laptop.

It was time to write that mission statement. In the end, it didn't take me long. I knew what I'd wanted to say. I studied my computer. The statement could probably use some tweaking, but on the whole I was satisfied.

I filled out the paperwork Harper had left for me and called Clayton. "Hi, this is Maddie."

"Oh, hello. Is there a problem?" he said anxiously. "You haven't decided not to take the collection?"

"No, I'm taking it. And thank you again for the opportunity." I drew in a deep breath. "I filled out all the paperwork. It will take a few months to get everything approved though."

GD hopped onto the counter and meowed.

"I expected that." Clayton hesitated. "You're sure about this?"

"Aren't you?"

"I'm sure I want to get that collection off my hands. I'm just not sure I want to burden you with it. I didn't realize—I spoke with your mother—"

"What?" My gaze flicked to the black crown molding. What was my mother doing talking to Clayton about my business?

"We ran into each other at the grocery store. She explained how complicated everything was. I didn't realize," he repeated.

"It's not complicated," I said. "Well, it's a little complicated. But I'm looking forward to the challenge."

And suddenly, I realized it was true. The fluttery feeling in my chest wasn't nerves; it was excitement. "If you're okay with waiting a few months for the final hand-off," I said, setting my pen on the counter. "I do want the collection."

"I can manage waiting," Clayton said. "As long as I don't have to go into that creepy warehouse again."

I laughed. "Now that I've got my own set of keys, you're off the hook."

He released a long breath. "Thank you. Let me know what you need from me, and I'll help any way I can."

"Thanks." We said our goodbyes and hung up. Then I made another call. This one took longer, but I hung up, satisfied.

Then I called Jason. It went to voicemail. "Hey," I said. "I have this weird idea... Is it possible that none of the obvious suspects we talked about did it? I was thinking about that party, and—"

CLICK. I checked my phone. His voicemail had hung up on me. Trying again, I got a *this-voicemail-is-full* message. I shrugged. Jason would call me back.

I shut off the lights, refreshed GD's water bowl, and left through the tearoom. Waitstaff and cooks clattered about in its kitchen.

I hesitated, the bag with the goblet in my hand. Adele looked busy. We could talk later.

I pushed through the heavy metal door at the back of the hallway and into the brick alley. My pickup was tucked behind the dumpster beneath Mason's apartment. I glanced up.

His windows were lit. I imagined Mason helping Jordan with his homework, the two pretending everything was fine. And it wasn't. If I was right, it would never be fine again.

"Belle, why'd you do it?" I muttered. Though now I had a fairly good idea why, it still made little sense.

I fumbled my keys from the pocket of my hoodie. A limo glided to a halt beside my pickup, blocking me in the alley. My stomach tightened.

Thane, in a black jacket and driver's hat, stepped from the black car. "Have you got the goblet?" He walked around the limo toward me.

"As a matter of fact," I said, heart thumping. "I have." I raised the bag.

He opened the passenger door to the long car and angled his head toward it. "Get in."

No. No *way*. "You know, I'm on my way to—"

He grasped my arm and thrust me inside.

I half fell across the seat. "Hey!" I straightened and checked inside the paper bag. I exhaled through pursed lips. Neither the goblet nor the box had been damaged by the rough handling.

The door slammed, shutting me inside. The door locks clicked.

On the black leather seat across from me, Mrs. Grandall raised a patrician brow. "Have you found the goblet yet?"

"Yes." I clutched the bag to my chest. There was no use denying it. But there was also no way I was going to hand it over to a murderess.

chapter twenty-nine

THE LIMO SMELLED LIKE new car. I didn't remember that smell from the first time I'd been inside. And I wondered—because it beat wondering if I was being kidnapped—if you could buy that scent in a bottle.

Mrs. Grandall was dressed for a kidnapping, in a black track suit. The white racing stripe down the side only slightly marred the evil villainess vibe. The cut crystal decanter from my first visit was gone, so I wouldn't be able to use it as a weapon.

I wasn't sure if I'd be able to bring myself to bludgeon her in any case. Hitting a white-haired lady went against my every instinct, even if she totally deserved it.

"Well?" Mrs. Grandall said. "Are you going to show it to me?" The limo moved forward, and the old lady swayed in her seat.

I swallowed. *Showing* it to her wouldn't hurt. *Play along.* I reached into the paper bag and extracted the box. I turned it so its glass cover faced her.

She frowned and smoothed the thighs of her workout slacks. "I approve of a display box, but why is the glass covered in those strange squiggles? They look trashy."

Trashy? Despite the fear slicking my skin, I nearly laughed. "They're protective sigils."

"What?"

"Magical symbols."

She huffed a laugh. "Do you really think those will stop that little man from stealing the goblet again?"

Sending a silent apology to Herb, I didn't respond. The sigils were designed to keep the curse inside the box. But I had a feeling she wouldn't respond well to that idea.

Her eyes narrowed. "Ah. They're not to protect the goblet. They're to protect people *from* the goblet."

"I *do* run a paranormal museum." I returned the goblet to the bag, its paper sides rustling.

"What do you think makes the goblet so dangerous?" she asked casually.

"Ah, it's unclear. Doesn't really matter," I gabbled. "I'll make up some story."

Her mouth pinched. "Strange. Your mother and the other bores in Ladies Aid seemed to be under the impression that you conducted meticulous research into your exhibits. Not that you... *made things up.*" She put the final three words in air quotes.

"I was thinking of sticking with the lucky goblet story."

"Story?" She pressed a button in the arm of the door. "Thane. Drive to Maddie's new warehouse. You know the one."

I swallowed. "The warehouse?" *The lonely, out-of-the-way warehouse?*

"I would think after losing it, you'd want to lock up that goblet." She righted her white wicker purse beside her. "Don't you?"

My head nodded like a bobble doll on a semi's dash. "Oh. Yeah. Right. I really do. Or I could just take it back to my museum." Where there might be people on the street. "I don't want to put you out."

"It's no bother."

I looked out the tinted window. We'd already left downtown. The limo had entered a more industrial area of garages and gas stations and fast food joints. Their neon signs blurred in the glass. No one walked along the sidewalks.

I settled back on my seat and smiled. "So how was your day?"

"Eventful."

"Oh?"

"A young woman attempted to blackmail me."

I forced an uneven laugh. "What? That's crazy."

"Isn't it, though?"

"And you told her to pound sand?"

"Something like that." She leaned the purse against her leg.

A chill iced my gut. *Belle.* What had she done? And what had Mrs. Grandall done to her?

"I hate the idea of blackmailers," I said rapidly. "But I guess that sort of thing is common in politics and such. Which you're not involved in, so..." Would it be weird if I didn't ask for more details?

Yes, it would be weird. "What did she think she could blackmail you over?" I continued.

Mrs. Grandall flicked a white speck from the sleeve of her black jacket. "She seemed to think I had something to do with that young man's death."

"Chadwick?" I yelped. I shouldn't have asked. I *really* shouldn't have asked. "That's crazy."

I was saying crazy too often. Did she think I thought she was crazy? Because I *did* think killing someone just to preserve your ancestor's reputation was nuts.

Of course for someone like Mrs. Grandall, it had been more than her ancestor's reputation. Her identity as first lady of San Benedetto had been on the line. And identity loss could feel like death.

Maybe that's why I'd been struggling so hard against losing mine as the plucky owner of a quirky museum. Not that my ego issues mattered when faced with the possibility of *real* death.

What had she done to Belle? *Look normal.* I stretched my mouth.

"Do you *really* think it's mad?" she asked. "The idea of me killing a strapping young man like Chadwick?" The limo braked sharply, and she rocked backward against the black leather.

"Of course," I babbled. "I mean, no offense. You've been working out, and it shows. But what did this woman think you did? Crack him over the head with a candlestick in the drawing room? Ha. Ha ha."

Oh. Mrs. Grandall *could* have actually done that. I'd figured she'd let Thane do the dirty work. It would explain why she'd decided to adopt her trainer. As heir apparent, he now had millions of reasons to keep his mouth shut. But maybe he'd just helped with the cover-up. I swallowed.

And Belle had been at the party that night, upstairs. She could have seen everything. If Belle was attempting blackmail... My heart twisted. *Mason.* Belle was not the person he'd thought she was. What would this mean for their son?

"I suppose this woman thought you killed Rea Bobberson too?" I asked lightly. I pressed my palms into the buttery leather seat to keep them from giving away their trembling. "I mean, how did she think *that* happened? Did your personal trainer strangle her for you?"

I bit back a curse. *That* was feasible too. Why was I talking? *Shut up shut up shut up.* "Did Ladies Aid also tell you I have this wild imagination? It's why I've been so successful with the museum."

"Not *that* successful." She studied her manicured nails, a soft, pink opal. I hadn't notice before how much they looked like talons. "Obtaining this massive donation was more a matter of luck, wouldn't you say?"

"I don't know. I think we make our own luck by getting out there and getting at it."

"And solving crimes?" She cocked her fluffy white head.

"Ah... Clayton *was* grateful when I cleared up—I mean helped clear up those murders. But, you know, if you want to call it luck, that's fine too. The point is—"

"The point is, you have a habit of sticking your nose into other people's business."

"I don't know if I'd put it like *that.*"

She folded her wrinkled hands in her lap. "It is exactly how I would put it." The limo bumped over the train tracks, and we swayed.

I reached up and grasped a handhold for balance. "Well, good on you for telling that woman to take a hike."

"Hm." She adjusted the white purse beside her. "Aren't you curious about who the woman was?"

I shook my head. "I'm sure I don't know any blackmailers."

"Don't you?"

"Nope. Can't think of a one. My friends are all straight arrows. They say that you're the product of the five people closest to you. Or maybe it's the seven closest. Anyway, I try to be around smart, good people. Like my boyfriend, Jason Slate. You know? The detective? We actually have a date tonight. I should give him a call to let him know I might be late." I lifted one hip and reached into the rear pocket of my jeans.

She pulled a silver gun from the side pocket of her wicker purse and aimed it at me. "Put your phone on the floor."

Palms slick, I released the phone, and it thudded softly to the limo's carpeted floor. "What's ah... What's going on?"

"Stop playing dumb. I've spoken with Herb and know *exactly* what you know."

My insides clenched. She'd spoken to... *Oh, no. Not Herb too.* "What did you do with him?" I croaked.

"You'll find out soon enough."

Oh, God. I'd been making fun of Herb's paranoia, and he'd actually been attacked by a crazed collector. He'd never let me live this down—if we both stayed alive long enough for him to guilt me over it. "What—?"

She raised the gun higher, giving me a prime view down its barrel. "Be quiet."

My gaze telescoped to the gray, metal cylinder. I shut up.

We continued past vineyards and barns and drove into a parking lot. The limo pulled up beside the warehouse.

The driver's door opened and slammed shut. After a moment, the passenger door opened. Mrs. Grandall nodded to me. "Get out. Slowly."

Crouching, I slithered from the limo. Thane grasped my arm and yanked me to standing. The big man frog marched me to the warehouse's metal door.

"Open it," Mrs. Grandall said, her purse over one arm. With her free hand, she kept the gun trained on me.

Damn, did it have a pearl handle? It *did.* Mrs. Grandall had to be the most elegant murderess I'd encountered. This did not make me feel better. Elegant people tend to focus on the details.

Hands shaking, I fumbled the keys from the pocket of my hoodie. I unlocked the warehouse door and pushed it open.

Thane prodded me inside. He and Mrs. Grandall followed. I switched on the overhead lights. They clicked on one after the other, illuminating the long aisle with cones of jaundiced light.

"The records," she said. "Where are they?"

"The office is that way." I nodded down the aisle of carrels.

"Then take me there. Thane, get the things out of the trunk, will you?"

The big man nodded, turned, and retreated before I could wonder too much about what kinds of things he was getting. She waggled the gun at me.

Taking the hint, I walked past the chicken wire walls caging paranormal artifacts that were no help at all. Even if Clayton's father had collected a cursed gun, it wouldn't be loaded. And if there were any cursed spears or staffs, I hadn't noticed them earlier.

"I suppose it was Thane who attacked me at the Mud Run site?" I asked. There probably wasn't much point to keeping her talking. But I *was* curious.

"You were getting too close to the truth."

I flipped through the keyring. Keys rattling, I unlocked the door to the cage where Clayton's father had kept his office.

Mrs. Grandall followed me inside. Alas, she was too far behind me to attempt a tackle that wouldn't involve me getting shot first.

"The records for the goblet," she said, "if you please."

I did *not* please. But I opened the tall cabinet's drawer. Thumbing through the manila files, I pulled out the file labeled SAN BENEDETTO GOBLET. I extended it toward her. "Here."

"Set it on the desk along with your keys."

I laid the file and keyring on the rolltop desk.

"Now walk to the cabinet and put your hands on its top," she said.

I did as she said. The metal was cool beneath my palms. "Have you done this before?" I asked. "Or do you just watch a lot of crime dramas?"

She lowered her head and glared over her glasses. "I *read*. I don't waste my time with television. It rots your brain."

I didn't watch much TV either. And I really hated it that we had something in common.

She slipped the file into her purse and grabbed the keys. The wire door behind me rattled, and I glanced over my shoulder.

In the aisle, Thane carried a bound and gagged Belle over one shoulder. He dragged a similarly bound Herb behind him by the collar of the little man's jacket. "Where do you want them?" Thane asked.

"Oh," Mrs. Grandall said, "anywhere will do."

He released Herb and let Belle slide off his shoulder. The hairdresser grunted when she hit the concrete, and I winced. I wasn't feeling particularly sympathetic toward Belle at the moment, but that had to hurt.

Mrs. Grandall backed to the wood and chicken wire door. Closing it, she locked me inside the cage. "Let's go."

She and Thane vanished down the aisle. After a moment, the warehouse door clanged shut.

Herb opened his eyes and glared through the chicken wire at me. "Mmph." It was a miracle his glasses had stayed on through a kidnapping.

"What are you complaining about? We're alive." Which... wasn't exactly in keeping with Mrs. Grandall's modus operandi. I tugged down the hem of my navy hoodie.

I scanned the cage, looking for ways out. But there were no convenient gaps or tears in the chicken wire. I rattled the door.

An acrid scent burned my nostrils. Herb's eyes widened. "Mmph!"

I sniffed, and my stomach spasmed. *Smoke.*

They'd set the warehouse on fire.

chapter thirty

I GRIPPED THE CHICKEN wire and shook it, the crooked wires biting into my fingers. It was a fruitless gesture, and I swore. On the other side of the wire, Herb glared up at me from the concrete hallway.

"I *know*," I shouted.

Turning, I raced to the rolltop desk and yanked out the drawers. No keys. No wire cutters. I studied an ivory-handled letter opener and shook my head. *No good.*

The scent of smoke grew stronger, though that could have been my imagination. I shook my head. It wasn't my imagination. I wasn't that lucky.

I looked around the cramped office. The rolltop desk. Tall file cabinets. Fantastically flammable cardboard boxes.

The file cabinets. I hurried to the heaviest looking one, made of wood. Grasping its edges, I leaned into it, and it shifted. This would do.

I peered around the cabinet at Herb and Belle. "Roll away from this, will you?" I yelled through the chicken wire.

They inch-wormed and rolled to the opposite side of the aisle. I shoved the top of the filing cabinet. Achingly slowly, it tipped with a groan and crashed into the cage.

The chicken wire bowed outward, the cabinet sagging lower. Metal pinged, hooks that had held the wire in place for decades flying free. And then the cabinet stopped, canted at a forty-five degree angle.

I hurried to its side and swore again. The bottom of the chicken wire was still hooked into the wood planks. The cabinet had pushed out the top of the wire, but I remained trapped inside. I kicked the wire. I sat on the cabinet. It didn't budge.

"Mmph!" Herb said.

I pivoted to a nearby metal cabinet. Removing the cardboard boxes from its top, I dragged it three feet from the cage wall. I shoved it over. Chicken wire snapped from its hooks. The cabinet crashed to the floor with a satisfying bang.

I punched one fist in the air. "Yes." I pushed up the wiring and slithered through. Something caught my hoodie, and there was a soft tearing sound. I ignored it. I had plenty of hoodies back at the museum.

"Mmph!" Herb sat up.

"I've got you." I hurried behind him. His hands and feet were bound with zip ties.

"Son of a... I'll be right back." I crawled back into the office, this time getting a long scratch from the wire on one wrist. Good thing I was up to date on my tetanus shots.

Grabbing the letter opener off the rolltop desk, I returned to Herb. The smokey smell was definitely getting stronger, and I glanced up. Smoke coiled in the warehouse's high metal rafters.

I sawed the plastic ties at Herb's feet. They snapped, and Herb grunted. "Mmph."

"Yeah, yeah." I hurried behind him. More carefully, I cut through the ties binding his hands.

He wrenched off his gag. "They've set the warehouse on fire."

Thank you, Captain Obvious. "I know," I ground out. "Get help." I turned to Belle.

Herb raced down the aisle. I cut Belle's ties, and she pulled off her gag. "What—?"

"It's locked," Herb shouted.

I gulped a breath. Of *course* it was locked. Why would they make escape easy?

Herb raced past us. "The rear door!"

Belle and I looked at each other. She leapt to her feet and raced after Herb. I followed behind. There was a clang, and a gust of fresh, cold air tossed my hair. Behind me came a faint, roaring sound.

"It's open," Herb hollered, holding open the door.

Belle raced past him and outside. I skidded to a halt. Two fire extinguishers bracketed the metal door.

My gaze met Herb's. I grabbed an extinguisher and raced back down the aisle.

"Maddie," he shouted.

But I couldn't let this go without a fight. There was too much history here. The artifacts *mattered*. And I didn't want Mrs. Grandall to win.

Flames blossomed inside the cage by the front door. My skin heated, and I caught a whiff of kerosene.

Fire licked the sides of antique cabinets. I jerked open the cage—thankfully, this one had been left unlocked. Pulling the pin on my extinguisher, I aimed and fired, eyes burning.

A trickle of white foam emerged and dripped onto my tennis shoe. "Oh, come on!" In hapless fury, I pitched the cannister at the flames. It clanged to the floor.

White foam shot past me. "There are two more extinguishers by the front door." Herb stood at my side. Flames reflected in his thick glasses.

Coughing, I nodded, ran from the cage, and grabbed another extinguisher. The fire had spread to the cage next door, consuming a cardboard box.

I sprayed the box. Then I walked deeper into the cage, spraying through to the burning cabinet on the other side.

"I'm out," Herb yelled and coughed.

"There's one extinguisher left by the door."

My fire extinguisher died. I hurried from the cage. Herb blasted past me and aimed the last extinguisher at a flaming spirit cabinet. Nothing came out.

We stared at each other in horror. My arms hung limp at my sides, my heart thudding dully against my chest.

That was it. Even if we could contact the fire department, there was no way they'd get here in time to save the collection.

"We need to get out," Herb said. "We've done all we could." He grasped my hand. "Come—"

Fire retardant shot past us. Mason shoved Herb aside, and the little man released my hand. Mason played the extinguisher over the cabinet. The flames died down, then vanished.

Herb pressed the sleeve of his tweed coat to his mouth. "Thanks." He coughed.

"That was..." *Lucky. Amazing. Miraculous.* I shook my head. Suddenly my throat was too tight to speak. I wiped my eyes and told myself they were burning from the smoke. I coughed. "Good timing. How'd you find us?"

"I saw that guy force you into the limo and followed," Mason rumbled. "Sorry it took me so long. But Belle..." His broad shoulders dropped, his blond ponytail brushing the top of his black motorcycle jacket. Sirens wailed faintly outside. "The cops and fire department are on their way."

My chest constricted. *Belle.* "Mason—"

"I know," Mason said, his blue eyes arctic. "Let's get out of here." He strode down the aisle, and Herb and I followed.

I grasped Mason's wrist. "Wait. Thane and Mrs. Grandall are out there. They have a gun."

He shrugged. "Not anymore. They're long gone."

We emerged into the chilly night. Belle stood huddled by an oversized black pickup.

"You keep a fire extinguisher in your truck?" Herb asked.

"You have a truck?" I asked.

"You never know when you'll need one." Mason stopped beside the warehouse's open door.

I glanced at Belle. She looked away. The gag still hung around her slender neck.

Mason folded his arms. He didn't move toward her. He didn't look at her either.

I swallowed. "I'll go to the front and let the cavalry know what's going on."

Mason nodded. I strode around the corner of the metal warehouse.

"Uh, I'll go with you." Herb trotted after me.

"I thought you hated the police," I said.

"They beat domestic dramas," he whispered. "I thought those two were engaged?"

Not anymore, I thought numbly. Not if I knew Mason.

Things got busy after that. The fire department got there first. They broke the lock on the warehouse's front door, giving them easier access.

I watched anxiously while men in thick canvas overcoats ran inside with fire hoses. Water could be as destructive as fire, and I gnawed my bottom lip. Had we risked our lives for nothing?

Jason's gray sedan screeched to a halt. The door swung open, and he raced out. "Are you okay? What happened?"

I explained about Mrs. Grandall and Thane. Laurel's blue muscle car roared into the lot.

"Belle witnessed the murder—or at least enough to incriminate them," I said in a low voice.

Laurel strode to join us. "Well?"

"Belle was trying to blackmail them," I said. "She's okay." I nodded toward the rear of the building. "She's around back with Mason."

Laurel nodded. The detective jogged around the corner of the building.

"They came after me because I knew too much." Herb lifted his chin. "Not about the murder. At least, not about the recent ones. I knew too much about Vincenzo's disreputable past, so they abducted me and tried to kill me."

Two firefighters emerged from the warehouse. They dragged the burnt spirit cabinet behind them. Another carried out a charred box. He dropped it carelessly on the pavement, and my heart lurched.

"Careful!" I hurried to the box.

"We need to make sure everything that might start up again is completely out," a firefighter explained.

I gave a quick shake of my head. "Fine, but these are..." I opened the box. "Very old and valuable books."

The fireman shrugged and returned inside. Herb came to stand beside me. "You know... I might have a buyer for that burnt-out cabinet."

"Seriously?" I asked, scowling. He was trying to swing a deal *now*?

Herb raised his hands, his palms out in a defensive gesture. "I'm just saying, if you need the money? We could do one last deal before you destroy the paranormal object economy."

I rose and studied his soot-smudged face. "Herb, we've been working together for a long time."

Behind his glasses, his eyes narrowed. "If that means you want a bigger cut—"

I waved that aside. "You're one of the most knowledgeable people I know when it comes to paranormal objects."

"*One* of the most?" His brows lifted.

"I'm going to be busy with the business and marketing side of the new museum. But it's going to need a full-time curator. Someone to organize the exhibitions. How would you like the job?"

Herb's mouth opened. Closed. "What's the pay?"

"I have no idea."

"It's a deal."

I smiled.

chapter thirty-one

OUR MISSION: TO ENCOURAGE *and develop the study of mankind's interaction with the paranormal, to preserve and interpret paranormal artifacts, and to advance knowledge of the supernatural while stimulating fun and the imagination.*

Bowling pins clattered as I studied the statement. It was a little long. It could still use some tweaking. And I was sure Herb would have ideas for improvement. But on the whole, my new mission statement wasn't bad. I even sounded like I knew what I was talking about.

A shadow fell across my table, and I looked up. Jason slid into the booth beside me. "Hey." He smiled.

"Hey, back." I kissed him lightly and hoped the basket of fries in front of me covered the smell of smoke. I'd showered and changed, but the scent still seemed to cling. "How'd it go?"

"Grandall has lawyered up. But Thane is singing like a thick-necked canary."

I laughed at the mixed-up metaphor. "He confessed?"

"He said it was all her. She bashed Chadwick over the head with an antique iron."

"A family heirloom, no doubt."

"No doubt. Thane showed us where he buried the murder weapon. And no, you *can't* have it for your museum."

"That's all right," I said loftily and snagged a fry. "I've got quite enough exhibits to work my way through now."

He shook his head. "You shouldn't have gone back into that warehouse to put out the fire."

"Maybe not, but I did. I couldn't let all that history go up in flames without a fight."

Jason laid his hand atop mine and squeezed lightly. "I'd like to see you build some history of your own."

My face heated. What sort of history were Jason and I building? "Speaking of history... Was Chadwick trying to blackmail Mrs. Grandall?"

"Thane said no. Chadwick had purloined—"

"Good word."

"Thanks. He'd purloined a document from your warehouse indicating Vincenzo Benedetto wasn't the upright citizen people believed."

"Not if he'd killed Salvador Morales for his rancho," I said. We still had no more than strong speculation on that count. But speculation had been enough to drive Mrs. Grandall to murder.

A waitress in a poodle skirt breezed past carrying a tray of empty beer mugs.

"Salvador Morales's old property makes up most of downtown today," Jason said. "Grandall wanted Chadwick to keep his discovery quiet, but he refused. So she killed him." He shook his head. "It all happened over a century ago. What does it matter?"

But it did matter. The truth mattered. But that wasn't why she'd lost her head. "Her entire identity is tied up in being heir to the great Vincenzo Benedetto. She thinks of herself as first lady of the town," I said, my voice low and intent. "She couldn't lose that."

"No one would have thought less of her if her ancestor was a criminal. I'd be willing to bet every one of us has a lowlife or two in their family tree."

I laughed shortly. "After all the years she lorded her special status over everyone? Oh yes they would have. Not that that justifies what she did. I suppose she destroyed my documents?"

"*Your* documents?" Jason arched a brow. "You've gotten proprietorial fast."

I shrugged. "I've got a mission statement now. It changes things." I glanced around. The bowling alley was packed. A last hurrah?

"I'm sorry to tell you the answer is *yes*," he said. "Grandall destroyed the evidence. What she didn't realize was Chadwick had already scanned the documents and had a copy on his laptop."

A weight settled in my chest. "Which Belle stole?" She'd been carrying a black backpack when I'd seen her leave the party — Chadwick's laptop bag.

Jason nodded. "She was in the room next door sweeping up the night of the party. The door wasn't quite closed. She was about to tell them she was leaving. Then Grandall bludgeoned Chadwick with that antique iron. Belle saw it all."

"How'd she get his backpack?"

"After Grandall killed him, there was a bit of panicking. She and Thane left the room for a time. Belle took the opportunity, grabbed his pack, and left."

"And then she tried to blackmail Mrs. Grandall." *Why?* She'd had a good thing with Mason. How much money could have been worth throwing it all away? "Did Mrs. Grandall get his laptop?"

"Yes, but Belle had already copied everything to a cloud server. We've got it now."

Belle. My chest pinched. This was not going to be easy on Mason and Jordan. "What's going to happen to Belle?"

His chiseled face smoothed. "She's busy making a deal with the prosecutor."

"And you don't like it," I said.

"It's not my business."

"But you don't like it."

"I don't like blackmailers."

I didn't either. I especially didn't like that one was now permanently connected to my friends. No matter what happened to Belle, she was the mother of Mason's son. She'd always be part of his life.

I shoved away the basket of fries. I wasn't hungry anymore. "But I suppose the DA figures it's better to set a blackmailer free than a killer?"

Jason nodded. "Grandall is a prominent member of the community, and she's elderly. He'll need all the evidence he can get to win in court."

I jerked forward, my stomach pressing into the laminate table. "You don't think she'll get off? What about Rea's murder?"

"Grandall's claiming that was an accident. She had no idea Thane would take things so far."

"An accidental strangulation? With a curtain cord?" I sucked in a quick breath. "The prosecutor can't believe her?"

"Of course not. But her fingerprints are on the iron that killed Chadwick. We've got her for that killing."

I slumped in the booth and blew out my breath. I sure hoped they had her. "Did Rea know what Chadwick had discovered?"

Jason nodded. "Thane says at first, Grandall thought Rea was the woman blackmailing her, not Belle. She knew Rea had worked with Chadwick. And Belle had been stuffing anonymous letters in Grandall's mailbox. Grandall went to Rea's house to confront her. When Rea admitted she knew about Chadwick's research, it seemed to confirm she was the blackmailer. But after Rea was dead, the blackmail notes kept coming."

"Because they were from Belle, not Rea," I said.

He nodded, his expression somber. "Of course, Belle thought Grandall knew it was her the whole time."

"Which is why Belle was laying low. What a disaster."

Jason's head bent. "You're worried about Mason." His gold-flecked eyes seemed to darken.

"And their son. If Belle doesn't go to jail—I mean, she's still in Jordan's life. But she's kind of awful." *Mason...* What was he going to do?

"It's not your problem," he said gently.

"I know, but..." It worried me. Mason and I might not be dating, but I still cared. He was a good person and a good neighbor. He didn't deserve this. But life handed us all sorts of things we didn't deserve. We just had to learn to manage them.

"So why did you want me to meet you here?" He motioned around the bowling alley.

Yes, change the subject. I forced a smile. "I wanted you to be the first person to know the location of my new expanded paranormal museum."

His brow wrinkled. "Not... here?"

"Mr. Chang's agreed to sell the Wok and Bowl to the museum foundation. Once the foundation exists. Which it will soon. The nonprofit status is a sure thing. We're just waiting on some paperwork from the state." And that would take some time.

"You're moving into a bowling alley," he said flatly.

"It's perfect. It's got that elevator down to the alleys making the place handicapped accessible. All I'll need to do is add some walls. And new flooring. But basically I'm buying a giant box that I can do pretty much anything with for not too much expense. And it's downtown. It's not on Main Street, but it's close enough."

Jason nodded. "I get it. I'm surprised you didn't tell your mother first, what with Ladies Aid being so involved."

I scowled. "Are you kidding me? She already knows, and I *didn't* tell her." There were no secrets from Ladies Aid. They'd known almost before I had.

"What's going to happen to the old museum?" he asked.

"Adele's expanding the Fox and Fennel. She's going to leave a little paranormal corner for a while though to help promote the new museum."

"And the secret door?"

"I'm moving it here. I want the museum to be more... interactive."

His golden eyes narrowed. "What have you got planned, Maddie Kosloski?"

I smiled. What did I have planned? *So many things...*

Note from the Author:

I borrowed much of the language in the letter from Francesco to Maria from a wonderful website called the Victorian Web. You can view the original letter, which is considerably more pious and less murdery here: Victorian Web. < >. Web. Date viewed: October 25, 2022.

<<<<>>>>

Click here to get your copy of *Sins of the Sarcophagus* so you can keep reading this series today.

Denial ain't just a river in Egypt...

Maddie Kosloski is about to unveil her new, expanded museum. But when the corpse of a local building inspector is discovered inside her prized Egyptian sarcophagus, Maddie's plans are thrown into disarray.

A modern mummy isn't all she's got on her hands. Running a non-profit paranormal museum is no get-rich-quick pyramid scheme. Maddie has stakeholders, more employees, and now donors to placate. Can she balance their demands *and* an off-the-books murder investigation?

Maddie must race against the clock to unearth a criminal more cunning than the Sphynx. But will the cost of unveiling this killer be more than she's willing to pay?

If you love laugh-out-loud mysteries with heart and a touch of the paranormal, you'll love *Sins of the Sarcophagus*, book 9 in the Perfectly Proper Paranormal Museum series of novels. (Especially since it wasn't written with AI).

Get cozy with this puzzling mystery today! Read this twisty cozy mystery!

Turn the page for a sneak peek of Sins of the Sarcophagus!

Sneak Peek! Sins of the Sarcophagus

Spirit Cabinet

USA, *circa* 1860

The spirit cabinet illusion was pioneered by the Davenport brothers, two fraudulent mediums active during the height of the spiritualist movement in the 1850s and '60s. This box illusion involved the brothers seating themselves inside a custom-made wooden cabinet the size and shape of a wardrobe. Once inside, they were bound by audience members. And then the cabinet's doors were closed.

Now hidden from view, the brothers were able to free themselves and start the show. Musical instruments would be played by "the spirits." Objects, including pale, disembodied hands, would appear from holes in the cabinet as if from the aether. Their 19th century audiences, unused to magic acts, believed the spirits were at work. When the doors were finally opened, the brothers would be seated again, their hands and ankles tied.

Other mediums copied the Davenport brothers' act before their trick was exposed by an amateur magician in 1865. This cabinet is an example of such a copy.

The second spookiest place in San Benedetto is the Ladies Aid Lodge. And I'm pretty sure I'm *not* the only person who feels this way.

Butterflies churning my stomach, I scanned the wide meeting hall, filled with chattering guests. Silken banners with cryptic symbols hung from the walls. Those belonged to Ladies Aid. Everything else was my museum's.

A terminal optimist, I'd planned on holding our soft opening inside the actual Paranormal Museum. But a hiccup with the town's building inspector schedules made that impossible. And since there was no use dwelling on what I couldn't control, I'd moved on to holding it at the Ladies Aid Lodge.

A camera flashed at the Spiritualist exhibit, briefly brightening spirit cabinets and talking boards. People wandered through the 20th Century Occultists exhibit featuring photos, books, and Tarot cards.

Herb, my new curator, expounded to a group of reporters beside the Debunking Mediums Exhibit. The little man adjusted his coke bottle glasses and motioned expansively toward a vintage Houdini poster. A reporter ducked beneath Herb's arm, and I bit back a nervous smile.

It was the Egyptian magic exhibit that had the most gawkers. No surprise—who didn't love a mummy? Not that I had an actual mummy—just the sarcophagus.

Naturally, it was cursed. If an object wasn't haunted, accursed, or unholy, it had no place in my museum.

"Excuse me, Miss," a masculine voice rumbled. "Do you have a permit for this event?"

I flinched before recognizing the voice. "You're hilarious as a heart attack," I said dryly.

My tall, dark and handsome boyfriend, Detective Jason Slate, grinned down at me. "Too soon?"

I laughed and tugged the lapels of his charcoal suit jacket, drawing him closer. "Not in your case."

Getting a permit for pretty much anything in California was a long, random, and expensive process. I'd been on the wrong end of that process trying to get the new museum up and running.

But I couldn't do anything about that now, and Jason was tall and solid and *here*. My gaze softened, my heart expanding at his presence.

Jason bent to kiss me, and I inhaled the scent of his spicy cologne—nice, calm, predictable, just like our relationship. Our lips touched.

A camera flashed, and I pulled away, embarrassed. Neither of us were into PDAs. Besides, the point of this soft opening was to gin up publicity for the new, expanded museum, not my social life.

I'd recently received a donation of such mind-boggling size I'd had to upgrade. Gone was the adorable little paranormal museum beside my friend's tearoom. Now we were a non-profit.

We'd snatched the local bowling alley from under some developers to turn it into the new paranormal museum. We'd kept one of the lanes—urban legend claimed it was haunted. I might not be able to stop change, but I was going to preserve what I could.

The change had forced me to step up my game in all sorts of unsettling ways. More staff, more professionalism. Many of the new objects in the museum were valuable and needed special care.

My newest employee, Chelsea, stalked toward us in a fitted little black dress. Her eyes narrowed, accentuating the cat eye liner. "Maddie, someone's spilled liquid at the base of the sarcophagus. I *told* you we shouldn't have brought it here. It's too fragile." The young woman flipped back her sleek, brown hair.

My stomach tightened. The sarcophagus wasn't *that* fragile. But it *was* old. Regretfully, I stepped away from Jason. "I'd better take care of this."

"I'll manage the crowd," he said somberly. But his eyes, toffee flecked with gold, twinkled.

On tiptoe, I kissed his cheek. Then I hurried toward the Egyptian display, grabbing a stack of napkins off the food table along the way.

A folding wall painted like an Egyptian tomb formed a backdrop for the closed and upright sarcophagus. Dusty wooden crates, straw and pottery spilling from them, lay scattered as if a tomb raider had just blown through. A black basalt Anubis statue as tall as Jason (six-foot-two) loomed over the display. The only modern element was a pedestal with a QR code for the audio tour.

The sarcophagus stood on a metal stand like one would use to display an ornamental plate. It tilted the wooden case back and off the floor. A muddy painting of a grim-looking ancient Egyptian with long, black braids glowered from the sarcophagus's lid.

I blotted the cool water puddling beneath the case. It was Chelsea who'd recommended keeping the sarcophagus off the floor. I'd been skeptical, but now I was glad the younger woman had been so insistent.

Our new registrar—responsible for the care and upkeep of the collection—knew her business. Her youthful expertise was more than a little intimidating.

"The Rosicrucians will be jealous," my mother purred. She studied the back of the sarcophagus and its painting of Maat, Egyptian goddess of justice.

I straightened, crumpling the napkins in my hand. "We're not in competition." The collection of Egyptian artifacts at the Rosicrucian museum in San Jose put ours to shame. But the Rosicrucians, as delightfully occult as they were, could keep their paws off my cursed sarcophagus.

My mother's mouth quirked. She wore white slacks and a blue denim shirt. Her favorite squash-blossom necklace, the same color as the silvery threads in her cropped hair, encircled her throat. "I know for a fact they offered to buy your Egyptian collection."

I rolled my eyes. Of *course* my mother knew. She was the co-president of Ladies Aid. They knew everything that happened in our small central-Californian town.

She plucked a stuffed mushroom off her gold paper plate and nodded toward the long table in front of the dais. "The new caterer is amazing. I'm glad you're supporting local businesses."

The red-haired caterer, Alex, sliced ham off the bone. He scooped warmed peppers from a chafing dish and assembled a mini sandwich.

My stomach rumbled. I loved ham sandwiches. They reminded me of lunches with my father, who'd died years ago. But I'd been so busy I hadn't had a chance to sample the food.

"Of course," my mother continued, "Melanie's catering will be considerably more upscale."

I bit back a sigh. Melanie overachieved at overachieving, including in her romantic life. She was marrying a glamorous Italian count next month.

I loved my sister, but Melanie's wedding plans had gone light years over-the-top. And if that sounded like sour grapes... I'm ashamed to admit it was. At least I'd be getting a Sicilian vacation out of the affair.

A commotion near the Debunking Mediums exhibit caught my attention. Herb flailed spastically.

"What is Herb doing?" my mother asked.

Herb's slight figure hopped sideways in a clumsy jig. He swung his arms above his balding head, his coat tails flapping.

Good question. "Ah... Summoning a spirit?" He didn't seem to be in physical distress, but... I stepped toward him.

Herb stilled and dropped his arms. His head bowed as if the performance was complete.

I shifted. So he wasn't having some sort of attack. But I moved toward him. He'd made a big transition recently too, shifting from paranormal collector to curator. "Mom, maybe I should...?"

A tall, muscular blond man in a leather motorcycle jacket, his hair pulled back in a ponytail, moved through the crowd. Mason's son, Jordan, trailed behind him, Mason in miniature. The pre-teen's shoulders hunched, his hands in the pockets of his jeans.

I stopped in my tracks, my heart pinching. We hadn't spoken much since things had gone so badly with Belle, his fiancée and the mother of his child. She'd broken off the engagement and abandoned both Mason and their son. But if he was here—

Arctic eyes serious, Mason caught my gaze. He smiled, then bent and said something to his son. Jordan darted toward the food table. Mason strode toward us, and I stiffened.

Mason's motorcycle shop stood next door to my old museum. He and Jordan and Jordan's mother had lived above it. And I'd sort of been responsible for Jordan's mother no longer being in the picture.

My friend Harper Caldarelli stepped between us. "There you are." She brushed a length of dark hair off her shoulder. "The museum's killing it tonight. All of Town Hall is here."

Harper was dressed professionally in a sleek forest-green business suit that set off all her curves. But as a town councilwoman and financial advisor, she always dressed to impress. "Thanks to you." I glanced past her. Mason had stopped to talk to an elderly woman in a blue knit suit.

"And that includes the inspection department," Harper added pointedly.

I growled and refocused on Harper. If it wasn't for the inspectors, we'd be in the actual museum.

My mother nudged my arm. "It wouldn't hurt to make nice."

My scowl deepened. *Make nice?*

In my old career, I'd worked in developing countries. Getting things approved by government agencies was a matter of who you knew or who you paid. The corruption was a large part of the reason these countries were euphemistically called "developing" rather than "developed."

Harper blew out a noisy breath, her olive skin darkening. "It's not entirely the inspection team's fault things got delayed. The head inspector quit without a word to anyone."

"I heard he ran off with his new girlfriend," my mother said.

"The point is," Harper continued doggedly, "we're short staffed."

"We?" I quirked a brow.

Harper was smart and capable and hardworking. But I still found it mildly hilarious that my friend was now a town bigwig. In high school, she'd slipped a carp into a classroom's A/C vent over spring break. The result had shut down the room for days.

The corners of her mouth tipped upward. "Okay, *they*. But sort of *we*. And I got them to agree to send someone out tomorrow."

"Tomorrow's Sunday," I said, shocked. The inspectors never worked Sundays.

Harper's grin broadened. "Like your mom said, it doesn't hurt to make nice."

"I'll say hi," I grumbled.

"You owe me." A woman's voice rose angrily above the crowd.

The caterer hurried around the long table and touched a slender woman's elbow. She was about his age, in her mid-fifties, with curling brown hair. She seemed small and fragile beside the big man.

Head bent, the caterer said something to her. She stiffened and strode into the crowd. Mouth compressing, the caterer returned to his station.

My mother tsked. "Marital troubles."

"You know her?" I asked.

"Wynnona Cookson," my mother said, "your caterer's wife."

I hadn't even known he'd *had* a wife. Trying not to look impressed at my mom's intel gathering powers, I moved toward the Debunking exhibit.

A man in his forties, his hair prematurely white, stepped in front of me. "Nice crowd," Frank Frost said.

I extended my hand, and we shook. "Thanks again for sponsoring the event," I said.

Frank threw back his head and laughed, a great, rolling chuckle. "Are you kidding? A cryogenics-slash-cryotherapy company sponsoring a paranormal museum seemed a natural fit. Most people think what Frostova does is creepy."

I thought it was creepy. "Are you getting many takers for your cryotherapy?"

"You'd be surprised. I'm hoping our cryotherapy program will help get people used to us. We're the only company in the world that offers both types of life extension services."

Uncertainly, I nodded. I'd read our sponsor's brochures. Cryonics froze the body after death. Cryotherapy was a cold therapy that was supposed to offer health benefits.

I motioned toward the turquoise *Frostova* sign behind the Egyptian exhibit. "I think the sign turned out well. I hope you're happy with the placement."

"I like the juxtaposition—the hot sands of Egypt and the cool turquoise of Frostova. Moving the soft opening here was smart, under the circumstances. Now you've got Ladies Aid on your side too."

With my mother as co-president, I'd always had them on my side. It would be embarrassing if they weren't such a town powerhouse. "They want to support the local economy," I said vaguely.

"Any word on those permits?" he asked.

I grimaced. "I was just going to go make nice with the inspection team." I nodded toward a cluster of bureaucrats beside the catering table.

"You wouldn't believe the grief they gave me when I was setting up." He shook his head. "But Frostova got through it. Your museum will too."

"That's—"

A woman's scream spit the air. People muttered, the crowd shifting. Frank and I exchanged worried looks.

"Oh my God! He's real," a woman cried.

I pushed through the crowd and popped from between two men like a cork from a warm bottle of prosecco.

At the Egyptian exhibit, Jordan held the sarcophagus lid awkwardly against him. The top of the lid angled above his head, its base resting against the floor. A mummy stood stiffly inside the open case.

I frowned. I hadn't put a mummy in there. Who'd added the mummy?

"Put that back," Chelsea snapped, striding toward him. "You'll damage the lid."

The mummy's knees buckled. Loops of damp, white fabric sagged downward, exposing a man's gray face and staring eyes. The mummy tumbled onto the linoleum floor and rolled onto his back. More fabric pulled loose across his chest, exposing an SF *Giants* logo.

I stopped breathing. I think my heart stopped beating too.

That was no mummy.

"I just wanted to see inside," Jordan said weakly. He shifted the lid against his body.

Jason appeared at my side. Gently, he edged me sideways and knelt by the mummy. He pulled out his phone. "Maddie, get everyone back."

"But that's not—" I pointed shakily.

"Get everyone back," he repeated. "This is a crime scene."

Can't wait to read more! Order *Sins of the Sarcophagus*!

More Kirsten Weiss

THE PERFECTLY PROPER PARANORMAL Museum Mysteries

When highflying Maddie Kosloski is railroaded into managing her small-town's paranormal museum, she tells herself it's only temporary... until a corpse in the museum embroils her in murders past and present.

If you love quirky characters and cats with attitude, you'll love this laugh-out-loud cozy mystery series with a light paranormal twist. It's perfect for fans of Jana DeLeon, Laura Childs, and Juliet Blackwell. Start with book 1, *The Perfectly Proper Paranormal Museum*, and experience these charming wine-country whodunits today.

The Tea & Tarot Cozy Mysteries

Welcome to Beanblossom's Tea and Tarot, where each and every cozy mystery brews up hilarious trouble.

Abigail Beanblossom's dream of owning a tearoom is about to come true. She's got the lease, the start-up funds, and the recipes. But Abigail's out of a tearoom and into hot water when her realtor turns out to be a conman... and then turns up dead.

Take a whimsical journey with Abigail and her partner Hyperion through the seaside town of San Borromeo (patron saint of heartburn sufferers). And be sure to check out the easy tearoom recipes in the back of each book! Start the adventure with book 1, *Steeped in Murder*.

The Wits' End Cozy Mysteries

Cozy mysteries that are out of this world...

Running the best little UFO-themed B&B in the Sierras takes organization, breakfasting chops, and a talent for turning up trouble.

The truth is out there... Way out there in these hilarious whodunits. Start the series and beam up book 1, *At Wits' End*, today!

Pie Town Cozy Mysteries

When Val followed her fiancé to coastal San Nicholas, she had ambitions of starting a new life and a pie shop. One broken engagement later, at least her dream of opening a pie shop has come true.... Until one of her regulars keels over at the counter.

Welcome to Pie Town, where Val and pie-crust specialist Charlene are baking up hilarious trouble. Start this laugh-out-loud cozy mystery series with book 1, *The Quiche and the Dead*.

A Big Murder Mystery Series

Small Town. Big Murder.

The number one secret to my success as a bodyguard? Staying under the radar. But when a wildly public disaster blew up my career and reputation, it turned my perfect, solitary life upside down.

I thought my tiny hometown of Nowhere would be the ideal out-of-the-way refuge to wait out the media storm.

It wasn't.

My little brother had moved into a treehouse. The obscure mountain town had decided to attract tourists with the world's largest collection of big things... Yes, Nowhere now has the world's largest pizza cutter. And lawn flamingo. And ball of yarn...

And then I stumbled over a dead body.

All the evidence points to my brother being the bad guy. I may have been out of his life for a while—okay, five years—but I know he's no killer. Can I clear my brother before he becomes Nowhere's next Big Fatality?

A fast-paced and funny cozy mystery series, start with Big Shot.

The Doyle Witch Mysteries

In a mountain town where magic lies hidden in its foundations and forests, three witchy sisters must master their powers and shatter a curse before it destroys them and the home they love.

This thrilling witch mystery series is perfect for fans of Annabel Chase, Adele Abbot, and Amanda Lee. If you love stories rich with packed with magic, mystery, and murder, you'll love the Witches of Doyle. Follow the magic with the Doyle Witch trilogy, starting with book 1, *Bound*.

The Riga Hayworth Paranormal Mysteries

Her gargoyle's got an attitude.

Her magic's on the blink.

Alchemy might be the cure... if Riga can survive long enough to puzzle out its mysteries.

All Riga wants is to solve her own personal mystery—how to rebuild her magical life. But her new talent for unearthing murder keeps getting in the way...

If you're looking for a magical page-turner with a complicated, 40-something heroine, read the paranormal mystery series that fans of Patricia Briggs and Ilona Andrews call AMAZING! Start your next adventure with book 1, *The Alchemical Detective*.

Sensibility Grey Steampunk Suspense

California Territory, 1848.

Steam-powered technology is still in its infancy.

Gold has been discovered, emptying the village of San Francisco of its male population.

And newly arrived immigrant, Englishwoman Sensibility Grey, is alone.

The territory may hold more dangers than Sensibility can manage. Pursued by government agents and a secret society, Sensibility must decipher her father's clockwork secrets, before time runs out.

If you love over-the-top characters, twisty mysteries, and complicated heroines, you'll love the Sensibility Grey series of steampunk suspense. Start this steampunk adventure with book 1, *Steam and Sensibility*.

Get Kirsten's Mobile App

Keep up with the latest book news, and get free short stories, scone recipes and more by downloading Kirsten's mobile app.

Just click HERE to get started or use the QR code below.

Or make sure you're on Kirsten's email list to get your free copy of the Tea & Tarot mystery, *Fortune Favors the Grave.*

You can do that here: KirstenWeiss.com or use the QR code below:

Connect with Kirsten

You can download my free app here:
https://kirstenweissbooks.beezer.com
Or sign up for my newsletter and get a special digital prize pack for joining, including an exclusive Tea & Tarot novella, *Fortune Favors the Grave.*
https://kirstenweiss.com
Or maybe you'd like to chat with other whimsical mystery fans? Come join Kirsten's reader page on Facebook:
https://www.facebook.com/kirsten.weiss
Or... sign up for my read and review team on Booksprout:
https://booksprout.co/author/8142/kirsten-weiss

About the Author

I WRITE LAUGH-OUT-LOUD, PAGE-TURNING mysteries for people who want to escape with real, complex, and flawed but likable characters. If there's magic in the story, it must work consistently within the world's rules and be based in history or the reality of current magical practices.

I'm best known for my cozy mystery and witch mystery novels, though I've written some steampunk mystery as well. So if you like funny, action-packed mysteries with complicated heroines, just turn the page...

Learn more, grab my **free app**, or sign up for my **newsletter** for exclusive stories and book updates. I also have a read-and-review tea via **Booksprout** and is looking for honest and thoughtful reviews! If you're interested, download the **Booksprout app**, follow me on Booksprout, and opt-in for email notifications.

BB bookbub.com/profile/kirsten-weiss

g goodreads.com/author/show/5346143.Kirsten_Weiss

f facebook.com/kirsten.weiss

instagram.com/kirstenweissauthor/

Made in the USA
Monee, IL
26 May 2024

58974965R00125